BACK TO THE RED ROAD

The Hunt for Crazy Horse's Women

by Chandra Lahiri

DORRANCE PUBLISHING CO
EST. 1920
PITTSBURGH, PENNSYLVANIA 15238

Dorrance Publishing Co
585 Alpha Drive
Suite 103
Pittsburgh, PA 15238
Visit our website at *www.dorrancebookstore.com*

ISBN: 979-8-8892-5209-2
eISBN: 979-8-8892-5709-7

BACK TO THE RED ROAD

The Hunt for Crazy Horse's Women

ALSO BY CHANDRA LAHIRI:

Red Road Across the Great Plains

Available on Amazon and all outlets served by Ingram Spark (paperback and e-book). Check out *www.dawnvoyager.com* for more.

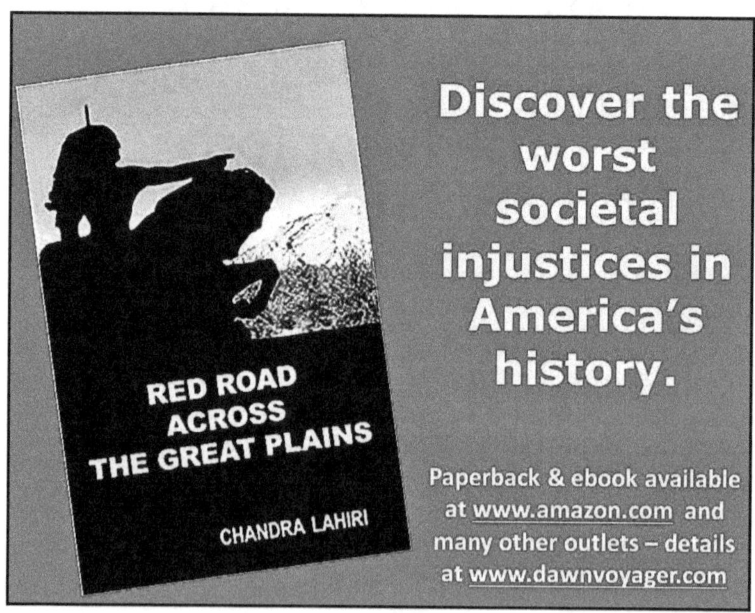

*Dedicated to my incredible family,
even though they never actually read either of my books!*

Keya, Shaon, Mayank, Laura, and Luca

HEARTFELT THANKS

This entire passion-research project would have remained just a waking dream, but for the amazing resources of the National Archives and Records Administration (NARA), and the incredibly patient, persistent and sincere efforts of one of the remarkable Archivists in particular, at NARA in Kansas City, Missouri. Stephen Spence gently encouraged my efforts, and patiently fielded my many requests for information and records over the course of almost three years, when we were all restricted at home by the Covid-19 pandemic. Not once over this long, trying period did he lose heart or patience, and it was, therefore, with considerable pleasure that my wife and I finally got to meet him at the unassuming NARA treasure-house in Kansas City. He turned out to be even more generous, helpful and likeable in person than I had already known him to be, from our long correspondence. Here's to you, my friend Stephen—your efforts cannot be overstated.

I would also like to thank my beloved wife, Keya, who joined me this time around, and patiently worked alongside me, hour after hour on those long days at NARA, combing through racks and racks of precious, ancient papers, handling brittle sheets with trepidation and reverence, searching for elusive clues to a jigsaw whose pieces were scattered to the winds more than a century and a half ago. As this is *my* passion project, and not hers, her efforts have my deepest appreciation and gratitude. The backbreaking effort was…well…truly backbreaking!

My sons, Mayank and Shaon, and daughter-in-law, Laura, were generous cheerleaders. Not reading my book is no indication that they did not believe in my, perhaps quixotic, quest for my personal holy grail!

I also owe a debt to the giants on whose shoulders I have ridden—the insightful, painstaking historians, the recorders of events of the Great Plains Nations. They are too many to name individually, but their books are listed in the Bibliography here and are well worth the read.

Any errors of understanding or interpretation are entirely mine, and for those, with all humility, I seek the forbearance of the People. I have tried my utmost, with honesty, dedication and an open heart, to tread the Red Road again, in search of lost souls. If I failed, it was not for lack of passion, belief or effort!

Chandra Lahiri
October 7th, 2022
Muscat, Sultanate of Oman

CONTENTS

BLACK SHAWL

(TASINA SAPE WIN)

TIMELINE : BLACK SHAWL

1840	Crazy Horse born at Rapid Creek
1841	Bull Bear killing by Red Cloud
1845	Black Shawl born (some claim 1943)
1846	Black Shawl born (per Census)
Sep 1851	Horse Creek / Fort Laramie Treaty
Aug 1854	Grattan Fight
Sep 1855	Bluewater Creek Massacre
1857	Great Teton Council at Bear Butte
1868	Bray : marriage with Black Shawl arranged
May 1869	Shooting of Crazy Horse by No Water
June 1870	Black Shawl married to Crazy Horse
1871	Incident of Big Bat's horses
1872	Daughter, Kokipapi/They Are Afraid of Her, born
Fall 1873	Daughter, Kokipapi/They Are Afraid of Her, died
1875	Wedding of Crazy Horse's half-brother, Bear Pipe
Jun 1876	Battle of Rosebud
Jun 1876	Battle of Greasy Grass / Little Bighorn
Jun 1876	Good Looking Woman died at Bear Butte
Aug 1876	Crazy Horse & Sitting Bull meet families, Slim Buttes
Q1 1877	Crazy Horse and Black Shawl wandering Black Hills
Feb 1877	Crook's peace mission through Spotted Tail
16 Apr 1877	Crazy Horse at Pumpkin Butte
27 Apr 1877	Crazy Horse north of Hat Creek Station
3 May 1877	Crazy Horse halted at Sage Creek
6 May 1877	Chief Crazy Horse comes into Fort Robinson
Summer 1877	Combing married. Iron Cedar living with Black Shawl
Aug 1877	Nellie Larrabee given to Crazy Horse
4 Sep 1877	Crazy Horse takes Black Shawl to Touch the Clouds
5 Sep 1877	ASSASSINATION OF CHIEF CRAZY HORSE
6 Sep 1877	Body taken to Camp Sheridan. Waglula and family transfer to Rosebud Reservation
Dec 1877-1886	Black Shawl living with They Are Afraid of Her at Thunder Butte, Cheyenne River Reservation
1878-1901	Waglula moves to Cheyenne River. 1878-1886 as Kills At Night; then as Breast of Female
1887-1899	Black Shawl living with mother, Red Elk, at White Clay, Pine Ridge Reservation. Mother died in 1898
1889	They Are Afraid of Her died
Dec 1890	Wounded Knee Massacre
1899-1900	Black Shawl living alone at White Clay, Pine Ridge
1907	Black Shawl died (as per Edward Clown Family)
Nov 1925	Black Shawl died (as per Death Certificate)
1927	Black Shawl died (as per brother, Red Feather)
1930	Black Shawl died (as per Ambrose)

GREASY GRASS

The urgent, desperate drumming of a horse's hooves shook the earth. Grass and twigs flew in all directions, as the single sleek blue roan flew past the massive, miles-long encampment, at a full gallop. The warrior, effortlessly riding bareback, like he was part of the animal, as did all his people, glanced anxiously in all directions, but especially into the trees edging out past the riverbank. She had to be here, somewhere—all alone, unaware of impending danger, blissfully searching for wild turnips and berries for his meal. There was no way she could know that Major Marcus Reno had already begun his charge across the Little Bighorn River, the one she and her people knew as the Greasy Grass, to attack their peaceful camps that had gathered for Chief Sitting Bull's great Sundance of the Northern Plains Nations a few short days ago. The warrior had to find his wife very quickly, and move her out of harm's way. As the preeminent war chief of his Lakota Nation, he had to reach the battlefront immediately, but for him the safety and wellbeing of his beloved wife took precedence. He simply had to find her, and find her fast. Time was running out rapidly.

Suddenly, Crazy Horse spotted her. Black Shawl was examining a bunch of wild berries, her back to the frantic activity along the riverbank, oblivious to the extreme peril that loomed large. The great warrior rode straight for her and, without slackening his gallop, slid over onto his horse's right side and scooped her up effortlessly. Black Shawl did not panic, as she knew only her husband was capable of performing this feat, without injury to either of them or to his horse.

The animal, instantly responsive to every nuance of Crazy Horse, wheeled around in a blur of speed, and carried the two back toward the farther reaches of the encampment, where all the other women and children had already been gathered for safety. They would shelter in what the soldiers called Squaw Butte, protected by the Elders, led by the great seer and redoubtable warrior Chief Sitting Bull, who was still recovering from having donated a hundred agonizing pieces of his own flesh to Wakan Tanka at the recent Sundance. They would be safe here, with him.

Having deposited Black Shawl in his care, Crazy Horse raced to his own tent and, still at a full gallop, leapt from the back of his father's hunting horse onto that of his own, much-loved warhorse, Inyan. That animal needed no commands, and the gentle pressure of the warrior's thighs sent him flying forward, heading for the battle with Major Reno. Inyan would, years later, be sacrificed, as customary, to accompany his master in the afterlife, faithful and beloved companion forever.

He arrived at the river to find that a very small group of Lakota warriors had already routed the cavalry and Reno's troop was in full retreat, back across the Greasy Grass River, harried by whooping Lakota. Old Waglula had almost shot Major Reno himself, who was saved only because a Crow Scout leaned across to him at the last minute and was killed instead. It was this action, spraying brains across his face, that panicked Reno into a full retreat. All the way across the water, soldiers continued to fall from their saddles, pierced through with arrows or shot by the obsolete guns wielded by some of the Lakota. Crazy Horse, arriving late, picked off a few stragglers. Reno, like Custer, had underestimated the ferocity of his opposition, without realizing just how few they initially were. Rapidly gaining the bluffs overlooking the river, he dug his force into a defensive position and would not move from there till the entire action was over, and the Lakota and Cheyenne camps eventually dispersed, anticipating the arrival of far larger, fresher forces under General Alfred Terry who, they knew, was on the march from Fort Abraham Lincoln, in the Dakotas. Reno would later be joined by the troop under Captain Frederick Benteen, who had been sent on a futile diversion by Custer sometime earlier, possibly to avoid having to share the "glory" and limelight when he routed these "savages." By then, Custer's eyes were firmly fixed on the Democratic Presidential nomination, slated for a few weeks thence in

Chicago. Prudence, tactics and the welfare of his men—even the direct orders of his superior, General Terry—were of secondary importance to his vainglorious ambition. It would be fateful hubris.

Reno's defeat was an early and unexpected victory for the Lakota. Realizing the situation was well under control, leaving his father, Waglula, and brothers, Combing and Bear Pipe, to chase Reno, Crazy Horse raced upriver to the next confrontation where, he was informed, Lieutenant Colonel George Armstrong Custer himself was trying to attack across another shallow in the river. This was the man infamous for always targeting Native women and children, while doing his best to avoid confronting the warriors, to use these soft, non-combatant targets as leverage to force the warriors to surrender without a fight. He was equally infamous for his overweening ego and abuse of young female captives, a man for whom the lives of his men were of less significance than his own vaulting dreams. Crazy Horse exulted at the thought of confronting this despicable cavalryman, who had once boasted he could defeat the entire Lakota Nation with just his 7th Cavalry. That challenge had just been accepted, and it was time to live up to his braggadocio.

As Crazy Horse charged up to the crossing point, he could see elements of the 7th Cavalry milling about in utter confusion in the middle of the river, at the place the wasicu called Medicine Tail Coulee. He realized that his people had already won this battle too. Custer had been riding arrogantly, well ahead of his column, crossing the river to attack the undefended families, as usual. His distinctive head of yellow hair made him easy to identify, and he was immediately shot dead by a warrior on the opposite bank, his body crashing off his horse into the shallow river. Custer was the first officer casualty of the Battle of the Little Bighorn, or the Greasy Grass Fight, as the Lakota knew it. Archeological evidence uncovered in later years indicates a disorganized rout, making it obvious Custer was no longer in command. It was only after some time, and more casualties, that his men were able to collect his body from the river, put it on his horse and retreat as fast as they could. At this stage, the retreat was probably led by his more gallant younger brother and aide, Captain Thomas Custer. Chased by warriors infuriated at the unprovoked attack on their women and children, they continued to race helter-skelter, not stopping to draw breath till they reached the little knoll that would one day be known, quite erroneously, as Last Stand Hill.

Custer's death, and the rout of his men, were witnessed by some of his own Crow Scouts, Goes Ahead, White Man Runs Him, Hairy Moccasin and, primarily, Curly, watching in grim silence from the bluffs overlooking the river, later named Weir Point (in honor of Captain Weir, who tried but failed to reach Custer to rescue him). The Scouts had tried desperately to signal a warning to the oblivious Custer. They knew what lay ahead for them, and they had been among the warriors who had strenuously and repeatedly warned Custer against attacking the giant encampment without waiting for Terry's reinforcements. As that would have meant having to share the glory, Custer ignored their advice. The U.S. Army, too, as part of its later investigation into the debacle, after General Terry finally arrived and relieved the besieged Major Reno and Captain Benteen, concluded that Custer was, almost certainly, killed at this point, and not on the so-called Last Stand Hill. The "boy general" finally had his day of reckoning, and paid the ultimate price for his hubris.

Crazy Horse watched the panicked retreat in disappointment but, being the unusually insightful war leader that he was, realized instantly that the battle was not over, now led by seasoned veterans like Custer's similar-looking brother and the courageous Captain Myles Keogh. After making a fearless solo charge right over Keogh's skirmish line, he saw Chief Gall and other experienced war leaders racing to take the 7th Cavalry on, in a frontal collision. He realized that they had left a huge crucial gap through which the troop could still escape. Without hesitation, and without looking back to see if any followed his lead, he galloped off to round the knoll and cut off any possible retiral. It says much for his sheer charisma and the awe the great Crazy Horse inspired that every warrior around him abandoned the tempting battle in front of him and followed his lead unhesitatingly, as usual without any commands or instructions needing to be issued, to attack up the back of the knoll. Among those accompanying him was his ever-faithful cousin, Chief Touch the Clouds. This crucial flanking action sealed the fate of the 7th Cavalry, which was wiped out to the last man, and all but one horse—Captain Myles Keogh's Comanche. The day was June 25, 1876, heavy with fate and foreboding. It was the high noon of the Lakota resistance, the final splutter of the bright flame.

It took just two hours for the Lakota and Cheyenne to exterminate Custer and his unit of the 7th Cavalry, and as the last of the 210 soldiers died, many throwing down their weapons and pleading for the mercy they had never shown the Natives, the women from the camps swarmed the field to exact their own revenge on the deeply hated soldiers. The Cheyenne women, in particular, were savage in their mutilation of the bodies, having vivid memories of the merciless slaughter of Little Thunder's innocent peace-camp on the Bluewater Creek by General William Selby Harney (derided by his own people on the East Coast as "Squaw Killer Harney"), despite the Chief's offer of an immediate, unconditional surrender. The only soldier whose body was not touched was Captain Keogh, whose exceptional bravery earned the respect of the Lakota and Cheyenne.

Custer received special attention from the women, who stripped him completely naked and rammed an arrow up his penis, a fact the Army would tactfully withhold from his widow, the formidable Libby Custer. Later, the vastly experienced, clear-eyed President (General) Grant correctly blamed Custer for the resounding defeat, though his balanced assessment was quickly drowned out by Libby, who expertly orchestrated a nationwide campaign of deification, which saw the creation of the unfounded myth of Custer's Last Stand and even the burial of the once-court-marshalled Colonel at West Point—while his men were quickly covered over where they fell, strewn across the killing field. She proved to be the Machiavelli of spin doctors. This story suited the U.S. Army as well, as it narrated the saga of how a valiant Custer had been overwhelmed by a vastly larger force of "savages", spreading a glossy mirage over the uncomfortable truth about a vainglorious, selfish field commander's blunder, resulting in his entire unit being destroyed, to the last man.

Black Shawl, along with the other women, watched the battle from Squaw Butte on the opposite bank of the river, acclaiming Crazy Horse and his warriors' resounding victory (per the Edward Clown family). After the dust settled, it is highly unlikely that she participated in the mutilations and looting of the bodies of the soldiers. Such vengeful actions were genuinely alien to her gentle nature. She was a healer, an expert with medicinal herbs, not a warrior, like a few of the other women actually were. She undoubtedly remembered the horrific Bluewater Creek Massacre but was not any sort of a vindictive person. Moreover, unlike the others, she remembered Sitting Bull's visionary warning, not to touch any of the soldiers' possessions.

She would have moved back to her own tipi, to prepare for the return of her tired and tense husband. Sitting Bull, too, would have waited for him in his tipi nearby. The battle was over, but the war, far from it. Major Marcus Reno remained stubbornly dug in, though he posed no further threat to the camps. Captain Frederick Benteen, with the other unit of the 7th Cavalry, having joined Reno, had also been neutralized. However, the great war leaders were keenly aware that General Terry was approaching with a much large force. While the warriors lusted to take them on immediately, the wiser heads of the leaders were conscious of the acute danger posed to their women and children.

After much discussion and debate, it was reluctantly agreed by all the Lakota and Cheyenne bands to break camp and disperse in different directions. Their point had already been eloquently made anyway with the head of the detested Custer. There would be one less candidate for the Democratic Presidential nomination.

While Crazy Horse and Sitting Bull, with their warriors, headed southwest into the Pryor and Bighorn (Shining) Mountains to divert the soldiers, they sent the women, including Black Shawl, children and elderly off east to the relative safety of the Northern Camps at Bear Creek, on the Owl River (Moreau River), with his ageing father, Waglula (or Worm), and his wives, Iron Between Horns, Kills Enemy and Red Leggins (Red Legs, in some records), as well as Crazy Horse's foster mothers, the sisters, Good Looking Woman and They Are Afraid of Her. Here, on the road, the wife of his half-brother, Bear Pipe, gave birth to a son, whom they named Comes Home Victorious, in honor of the victory at the Greasy Grass.

The Lakota and Cheyenne bands moved unhurriedly away, leaving a mound of bodies and gore for the soldiers to recover. The non-combatants, always easy victims for "Indian Killer" generals, would be safely out of the area, and it was agreed that they would rendezvous with the two Chiefs in a few weeks' time, at the Slim Buttes, near the Black Hills in South Dakota.

As they neared the Black Hills, one of Crazy Horse's adoptive mothers, Good Looking Woman, who was terminally ill, probably with pneumonia, continued to fade, anxiously tended by Black Shawl and her other family members. She was the sister of They Are Afraid of Her and Crazy Horse's birth mother, Rattling Blanket Woman, and after her suicide Good Looking Woman had come to live with Waglula to look after her sister's child. At a rest stop at Bear Butte, a fast-riding Lakota messenger caught up with them, with a present for her from Crazy Horse, a pouch of shiny silver coat buttons, captured from a soldier at the Little Bighorn. With a blissful smile at the gift from her beloved adoptive son, Good Looking Woman finally passed to the other side. She was buried in the traditional Lakota manner at Bear Butte, close to where her son had his youthful vision. She would not see Crazy Horse at the end. Black Shawl took part in the funerary ceremonies and prayers to Wakan Tanka. The coat buttons probably passed to her. Then, the convoy pushed on eastward.

After the Custer debacle, Generals Terry and Crook were unwilling to face the Lakota and Cheyenne in battle again, till they could build up overwhelming superiority in men and munitions. Crazy Horse successfully decoyed the soldiers all over the Bighorn Mountains on a futile chase, burning the grass behind him to deny forage to the soldiers' horses, before fighting an inconclusive running battle with General Crook and Captain Anson Mills in the Slim Buttes area (present-day Reva, South Dakota). Despite vastly outnumbering the warriors, Crook was, again, unable to defeat Crazy Horse, who was intimately familiar with the terrain and an innate master of guerilla warfare. There were no casualties on either side, and the Lakota families were safely out of the soldiers' reach. The 7th Cavalry's desperation to avenge the humiliating defeat on the Little Bighorn would have to wait till December 1890, when they would slake their bloodlust on another group of defenseless Lakota, mainly old men, women and children, led by a dying Chief Bigfoot (also called Spotted Elk, he was the brother of Chief Touch the Clouds) in a haunting river valley called Wounded Knee.

Struggling through the deep snow of winter, they were attempting to reach the Red Cloud Agency to get away from the unrest at the Standing Rock Reservation, caused by the killing of the revered Chief Sitting Bull by Lakota Scouts sent to arrest him on a trumped-up charge by the nervous and resentful Agent at the Reservation, James McLaughlin. In a strange twist of fate, his ill-treatment by his own people, for whose welfare he had selflessly dedicated his entire life, as well as his murder at their hands would eerily reflect that of his friend and brother-in-arms, Crazy Horse.

After two months, at the end of August 1876, Black Shawl and her family, along with Sitting Bull's family, were reunited with them at Slim Buttes, as planned, after General Crook suffered a brutal forced march through the Black Hills, back to Fort Laramie, almost losing his entire troop to starvation on the way. For the second time, he had failed to defeat Crazy Horse, having already suffered defeat at his hands on June 17 in the Rosebud River Valley, known to the Lakota as the Red Flower River, just a few fateful months ago, forcing him to withdraw all the way to Fort Fetterman, leaving Custer to his date with destiny.

In the bitter winter of November 1876, Colonel Ranald Mackenzie attacked Cheyenne Chief Dull Knife's village at the Red fork of the Powder River. The pitiful survivors fled to Crazy Horse's camp. He had barely enough food and shelter for his own people at this point but took them in, nevertheless. Black Shawl would have been one of those who welcomed and succored the survivors. Mackenzie's unprovoked attack on Dull Knife's village, and the strange lack of game that winter, convinced many of the Lakota leaders on the Tongue River to pursue peace. Crazy Horse, whose following at the time consisted of about 250 lodges, struggled with that concept and, according to Black Elk, Marie Sandoz' "strange man of the Oglala" began to act even stranger than usual. "He hardly ever stayed in camp," Black Elk would recall later. "People would find him out alone in the cold, and they would ask him to come home with them. He would not come, but sometimes he would tell the people what to do. People wondered if he ate anything at all. Once my father found him out alone like that, and he said to my father: 'Uncle, you have noticed the way I act. But do not worry; there are caves and holes for me to live in and out here the spirits may help me. I am making plans for the good of my people.'" By then, Black Shawl was far too ill to accompany him, as had been their wont. This was also the time of the failed peace meeting with "Bear Coat" Miles.

Recognizing a superior foe and hungering for the glory of "bringing him in," Lieutenant General Nelson Appleton "Bear Coat" Miles reached out to him, for peace. However, Crow Scouts at his Cantonment Powder River sabotaged the dialogue by breaking discipline and killing some of the peace envoys, dishonoring the safe passage guaranteed them by the General. Miles immediately disarmed and dismissed the Crows, but it did nothing to decrease Crazy Horse's distrust and anger. It would lead, with leaden inevitability, to a final, inconclusive fight between the two in early January. Once again, Fate could perhaps have decreed a completely different conclusion to their story, had those undisciplined Crow Scouts not sabotaged it.

Between January and April of 1877, Black Shawl, Crazy Horse and their village, now numbering less than 2000, restlessly wandered his beloved Powder River (Shifting Sands River) country, the scene of so many of his past triumphs. They eventually camped at Hanging Woman Creek, on the Tongue River, where they would remain till the portentous move to Fort Robinson the following year. Black Elk, Crazy Horse's cousin by marriage, destined to become a great visionary in later years, was with them and would later recall that Crazy Horse was deeply disturbed, spending a great deal of time wandering the wilderness, accompanied only by Black Shawl, praying to Wakan Tanka for guidance.

Not only was the Army rapidly encroaching on their lands and, having failed to defeat them militarily, was resorting to scorched earth tactics by wiping out the buffalo, on which they depended for sustenance, but his beloved wife, Black Shawl, was seriously ill, suffering from what would be diagnosed later as blood poisoning and the early stages of tuberculosis. His concern for her was deep and reflected the love and respect that had grown so strong between them. His prayers gradually became an almost desperate plea to Wakan Tanka. Black Shawl was looked after by Waglula's wife, Kills Enemy, but she, too, eventually became infected, and died later that year at Bear Creek.

The great Hunkpapa leader, his friend Sitting Bull, showed up in his camp at this time and announced that he was taking his people to refuge across the Canadian border, to "Grandmother's Land" as Queen Victoria's dominion was known to them. Crazy Horse sadly declined to join him; he knew it was even colder in Canada, and that could only make Black Shawl's illness worse. Sitting Bull went off, after they agreed to meet in the spring—but they would never see each other again. Crazy Horse's love and care for his wife, indirectly, put him on an apocalyptic path. What might the future have held if they had been able to accompany Sitting Bull?

Further resistance did seem futile to many of Crazy Horse's followers. During those three agonizing weeks in the harsh midwinter, whenever she physically could, only Black Shawl accompanied Crazy Horse, riding around the Powder River country, tending his ancestors' graves and praying, praying,

praying, vision questing (hanblechaya). It was the biggest spiritual crisis of his life.

Meanwhile, in the bitter cold, Black Shawl suffered even more acutely, from a coughing illness. She had had it before, but now it gradually got much worse. She also had badly swollen arms, indicating inflamed joints, reducing her ability to manage even her own household, let alone accompany him on his wanderings. Medicine men had no cure for this, hitherto unknown European illness, and Crazy Horse was advised to go to Dr. Valentin McGillycuddy at Fort Robinson. He did not believe in the white man's medicine, but his wife's suffering affected him powerfully. Because of this, he vision-quested with single-minded intensity and, it is said, was eventually granted Eagle healing powers. However, destiny would not give him enough time to transform from warrior to healer. This school of healing was continued through Peter Catches, father and son, on the Pine Ridge Reservation, till a few years ago, when the younger Peter passed away without an heir to hand the knowledge on to.

Black Shawl vehemently opposed Crazy Horse's Agency scheme, as her weakness did not diminish her love for him, and she knew his vision had forewarned he would die if he ever lived near soldiers. Crazy Horse was torn between his wife's worry and her illness. He had no doubt that, once he won his Agency, his life would be over. But it was the only way to save his wife and his people. He prayed for guidance. A pitiless destiny ground on relentlessly.

In February, when they were again in the Black Hills, General Crook persuaded Crazy Horse's maternal uncle, Spotted Tail, to undertake a mission to him, loaded with gifts and a peace offer, promising him the Powder River Agency that had been his only major demand. In return for this service, Spotted Tail was made Chief of all the Lakota by the Army, demoting Red Cloud. Black Shawl and Crazy Horse were again roaming the wilds at the time, and so Spotted Tail met with old Waglula and left the offer, along with lavish gifts, with him. Whether this absence was an intentional snub to Spotted Tail is unknown. However, concern for his wife's worsening health forced him to consider the offer more seriously than he otherwise might have. Before leaving, Spotted Tail warned those present in the camp that, unless they surrendered, Crook would attack them with the help of not only Crow and Shoshone scouts but also other Lakota and Cheyenne.

Negotiations began without Crazy Horse participating. His simple demand was for his people to be given their own Agency in his cherished Powder River country, as outlined in Lone Horn's original proposal from five years ago (he later named his camp near Fort Robinson, Lone Horn Camp). With great prescience, he also demanded no confiscation of horses or guns, so they could continue to hunt and not be dependent on doubtful Government food largesse.

Finally, Crook and Crazy Horse reached an agreement, with a few small compromises. After all, both Generals Crook and Miles desperately wanted credit for the great Oglala's surrender. Unfortunately, it would turn out, the offer was one Crook had no authority to make, and Congress later reneged on it. Whether Crook intentionally misled him or was himself let down by his Government is unknown. A few months after this, Crazy Horse, having pledged his word as a warrior, finally gave up the warpath, never to return to it. His life was effectively over.

Waglula agreed to surrender at the Spotted Tail Agency, and his elusive son sent word through his father that he would soon bring his camp of Oglala and Northern Cheyenne in to the Red Cloud Agency. The presence there of Dr. McGillycuddy clearly had a major influence on his decision.

Still smarting from his humiliating failure to defeat Crazy Horse at either the Rosebud Valley or at their Black Hills encounter and jealous of General Miles, Crook promptly agreed when Red Cloud, determined not to be outdone by Spotted Tail, volunteered to go out and hurry the Oglala leader along. Red Cloud was allowed to take cattle and other provisions with him, so Crazy Horse and his followers would not have to stop to hunt on their way in to the Agency, then located in Western Nebraska. Red Cloud found Crazy Horse on the trail to his Agency on April 27. "All is well, have no fear," Red Cloud assured him, "Come on in." Without hesitation, Crazy Horse laid out his blanket for Red Cloud to sit on and gave the older man his shirt as a symbol of surrender to him. As the admired mentor of his youth, Red Cloud's words still carried weight with him, despite the enmity and acute jealousy the older man now felt for the young warrior, whose reputation and respect among the Lakota and Cheyenne now quite eclipsed his own.

Turning themselves in, though, must have been agonizingly difficult for Crazy Horse and Black Shawl, who had always lived free, in the traditional

Lakota manner. Now they would become dependent on condescending handouts, of doubtful quality, and have to obey the instructions of the wasicu they had fought so successfully for so long. But he was determined to do what was best for his people, as he had his whole life.

Black Shawl's worsening condition finally made him think the unthinkable: surrender. Eventually, the Doctor would become so much of a friend as to be known as "Tsunke Witko Kola" (Crazy Horse's brother). It nudged the fateful decision toward the Agency of Red Cloud, rather than that of his and Black Shawl's uncle, Spotted Tail. It is said the good Doctor's great care for Black Shawl melted the fierce warrior's heart, and it is probably this that enabled the very ill Black Shawl to recover and survive decades more than Kills Enemy, who had contracted the same illness and died. Even on his last, portentous evening, Crazy Horse acknowledged this kola when he passed him on the way to the Guardhouse at Fort Robinson. And he would be one of the very few to be with him to the bitter end.

By mid-April, Black Shawl was much worse and Crazy Horse moved his camp to Pumpkin Butte, on the road to the Red Cloud Agency. Even at this point he was reluctant and paused here awhile to pray and meditate on the future awaiting his people. By the end of the month, he had moved closer, to Hat Creek Station, but still hesitated. That month, Chief Touch the Clouds and his brother, Roman Nose, surrendered at the Spotted Tail Agency. As a measure of caution, Waglula and his family were sent with them, and the June 1877 Census of Spotted Tail recorded "Crazy Horse Father" with four women (two girls?) and two boys. Crazy Horse would have sent Black Shawl, too, with them, but her crippling illness was the very reason for his coming in at all, and he realized Dr. Valentin McGillycuddy was her last hope.

In early May, he made a final stop at Sage Creek to allow the struggling Black Shawl to rest a little, before finally establishing his Lone Horn Camp, near Cottonwood Creek, on the bluffs overlooking Fort Robinson and the Red Cloud Agency. By now, the numbers were down to 145 lodges, containing 217 men, 312 women, 186 girls and 184 boys. On May 6th, the storied Chief and his band of warriors, including his dearest friend, He Dog, and ironically, his own Judas, Little Big Man, rode proudly into a Fort Robinson lined with awestruck crowds of both Lakota and soldiers. As one officer noted, it was no surrender but a triumphal march of the unbowed and undefeated. Waglula and his wives would move to Lone Horn Camp on May 30, as confirmed by Lt. Jesse Lee's letter to Lt. C. A. Johnson dated May 29, 1877.

Black Shawl was with Crazy Horse, as confirmed also by the diary of the Doctor's wife, Fanny, which recorded that he was called to her tipi the very next morning. "Dr. was sent for, to go to see the squaw. The instruments were used and Dr. [Munn] assisted. Got home at about eleven o'clock." Crazy Horse clearly lost no time in trying out the Doctor's medicine which was, after all, his main reason for coming into this Agency.

She was one of the "3 females" listed with him and Tall Bull in the *Crazy Horse Surrender Ledger.* As to who Tall Bull, or Long Bull, was, he could have been one of the delegates sent to accompany him in or, as Sees His Horse, one of the Chief's present-day descendants, explains, "It was not uncommon to live together with another family, regardless of social status, since this embodied Generosity, one of the cardinal Lakota virtues. The exact reason can only be guessed at, of course, but I would put it down to pragmatism. Perhaps Tall Bull simply didn't own a tipi at the time, or did not bring it on his trek south, and Crazy Horse and his wife welcomed their friends into their household since they had space to." Equally possible, in view of Black Shawl's condition, is that Tall Bull's wife was also suffering from tuberculosis and their isolated tipi was ideal for her, too. It is recorded that Black Shawl had her own Ration Ticket, though it has not survived to reach the National Archives.

Crazy Horse had set up his tipi at the far end of his camp, to ensure her illness did not spread to the rest of his people. As Black Shawl responded to Dr. McGillycuddy's treatment, a bond developed between them, with his visits almost turning into social calls. However, curiously, Fanny's diary always refers to Black Shawl as "the squaw" rather than by her name. She also stated that Black Shawl died shortly after her husband and was buried with him—a claim that is patently incorrect, as Black Shawl was documented to be alive and well long after that time. It is not clear if the usually level-headed Fanny resented his growing bond with the legendary Chief and his family.

At any rate, Black Shawl continued to recover under Dr. McGillycuddy's care and her husband's devotion. As she got stronger, his deep-rooted distrust of the wasicu lessened slightly, and on May 26 he even agreed to his only-ever interview, with *The Chicago Times.* The Press, in those days, reported wildly inaccurate stories about his "four wives" and "numerous progeny," probably confusing him with Waglula, then also called Old Man Crazy Horse. Black Shawl, as was her nature, maintained a very low profile, as is evidenced from her complete absence from contemporary Press or military reports and correspondence. Life seemed to be settling down for the couple—but fearsome thunderclouds were already darkening the horizon, their fires ably banked by the jealous Red Cloud and the resentful Crook.

MAYHEM TO MATRIMONY

The jealous shot that injured Crazy Horse shattered the unity of the Lakota world and brought into the open the festering friction between the Red Cloud camp and that of Crazy Horse. As in a Shakespearean tragedy, for the love of a woman their world was rend asunder.

The murderous bullet fired by No Water, though not fatal, shattered Crazy Horse's jaw, leaving him in great pain. However, there was little that could be done to help him in a hunting camp. Fortunately, such news travelled fast, and the next day his maternal uncle, Spotted Tail, arrived at his camp with his own niece, Black Shawl, a notable healer with herbs, and she immediately set to caring for the injured man.

Born in 1845 (or in 1846, as per the Census or, more unlikely, in 1843 as per Hardoff), she was of the tiyospaye of Chief Big Road, born before the Horse Creek Council/Treaty of Laramie of 1851 and probably after the great cholera and smallpox epidemics. Her father, Good Hawk, was an Oglala Lakota, and her mother, Red Elk, a Sicangu Lakota, most likely a sister of Chief Spotted Tail. Her brother was Red Feather and her sister was Makes Alive/Red Elk/Iron Horse. She also had at least one nephew, from her brother, that we have a record of, Young Red Feather. Another, Makes Alive, who lived with them for two years at White Clay, could possibly have been a son of her sister, though there is no way to be certain. The rest of the family have vanished into oblivion. Between Black Shawl and Crazy Horse, they had close familial ties to three of the seven Lakota groups—Oglala, Miniconjou and

Sicangu—though their own people would let them down in the end.

Before he became Chief, Spotted Tail was Jumping Buffalo, of the tiyospaye of Chief Big Road. From Spotted Tail's five wives, Black Shawl had more than 28 cousins. Their last recorded direct descendant was John Spotted Tail, the great-great-grandson of the famous Sicangu Chief. Being such a close relative, it is all but certain that in her childhood and youth, Black Shawl and her family lived in and travelled with Spotted Tail's village.

Black Shawl was a little girl of six years when the first Treaty of Laramie was signed, at Horse Creek on September 17, 1851. She would have remembered this as it was a momentous event and there would have been much discussion and celebration in her village.

The storied Fort Laramie has a colorful history. It was founded in 1834 by the famed Mountain Men, William Sublette and Robert Campbell, as a trading post on the Laramie River, and they called it Fort William. They eventually sold it to the Rocky Mountain Company who, in turn, sold it on in 1836 to the American Fur Company. With its immense resources, this firm turned it into a major trading post. In 1841, they went further and erected a newer Fort John, later commonly referred to as Fort Laramie. Worryingly, in the 1840s the newly opened Fort Platte a mile downriver started offering serious competitive heat to the Fort John trading business. However, as fortune would have it, in 1845 Fort Platte was abandoned and locationally advantaged Fort John flourished again, especially with the Gold Rush having begun. It even became a major station for the Pony Express, which itself would become the stuff of sagas. By this time, it was invariably referred to as Fort Laramie. The U.S. Army acquired it from the American Fur Company in 1849 and officially renamed Fort John. Among other things, they brought the telegraph with them and consequently the legendary Pony Express rode into the sunset.

Finally, in 1890 Fort Laramie was sold off by the U.S. Government at a public auction. Nothing remains today of the first Fort Laramie, but some structures from the Army period, such as the Post Headquarters, survive as stubborn reminders of the once legendary outpost where so much history was created.

Three years after the Horse Creek Council, when Black Shawl was just nine years old, she most likely witnessed the Grattan Fight on August 19, 1854, at Chief Conquering Bear's (also known as Matho Wayuhi/Matoiwa/Brave

Bear/Scattering Bear) camp, near Fort Laramie. The wasicu had, in 1851, for their own convenience, made him Chief of all the Lakota, to his considerable bemusement, as he knew the Lakota only answered to the chief of their own band, and had himself never sought such a meaningless title.

On that day, however, a young and inexperienced Brevet 2nd Lieutenant, John Lawrence Grattan, decided he would teach the Lakota a lesson for harboring a Miniconjou guest who had killed a cripped, old, straggling cow of some passing Mormons. He led 29 heavily armed men into their camp, with a hubris that strikingly foreshadowed Custer's.

Completely ignoring the peaceable Chief Conquering Bear's explanation of Lakota hospitality, which forbade the handing over of their guest, as also his generous offer of compensation from his own herd, he brashly ordered his troops to open fire on the peaceful camp full of non-combatants. The first shot hit the Chief himself in the back, mortally wounding Conquering Bear. This infuriated his camp and the warriors immediately retaliated, killing all but one of the soldiers, the survivor allowed to return to Fort Laramie with a cautionary tale. Spotted Tail (Sinte Galeska), the Chief's first cousin, was one of the leaders of this fight. It would, however, be said of him later that though he fought well, his diplomatic skills were even better. Black Shawl would have been with the camp when it left the Fort under its new chief, Little Thunder (Wakinyan Cikala). Spotted Tail was to become his closest and most trusted deputy and advisor.

The new Chief was also a believer in peace, despite the actions of the feckless Grattan, and he kept his people away from the wasicu over the next year. However, again, fate would have it otherwise. Encamped on the Bluewater Creek, near what is today the Ash Hollow State Historical Park, in September 1855 his camp was ruthlessly attacked by the infamous General William S. Harney. Ignoring Chief Little Thunder's offer of an immediate, unconditional surrender, he set about butchering as many of them as he could, which clearly had been his intent all along. Eighty-six Lakota were killed and seventy captured, including Spotted Tail's wife and daughter. A severely injured Spotted Tail managed to escape. Later, many of Harney's soldiers would parade the private parts of their victims, especially female, through the streets of Denver as trophies. The Army chose to ignore this infamous behavior. The survivors, whether they narrowly escaped or were taken prisoner and later released, included Black Shawl and her family. In an ironic twist, it is likely this massacre was witnessed from afar by a youthful Crazy Horse, who would never forget it or forgive the wasicu and eventually become their worst nightmare. His dear kola, Little Hawk, was the nephew of Spotted Tail's brother, Little Hawk, tying Crazy Horse even closer to this wounded family— and making Spotted Tail's attitude toward him in the end days even stranger.

Their thirst for revenge for the foolish Grattan not sated, the U.S. Army held their Bluewater prisoners as hostages, pending execution, unless Spotted Tail and the four other leaders of the Grattan Fight (Grattan Massacre to the Army, despite Grattan's heavily armed troops having initiated the completely uncalled-for conflict) surrendered. In October 1855, realizing their loved ones were in serious peril, Spotted Tail, head held high, led the four others to Fort Laramie, from whence he was sentenced to prison at Fort Leavenworth for almost four years.

After his apparently amiable interactions with the officers and guards there during his incarceration, on his release he was a changed man. He had seen the might, and countless numbers, of the wasicu and was convinced peaceful coexistence was now the only option left to them. Black Shawl and her family would have been present for his surrender, either as prisoners or, more likely, living in their camp near the Fort. This personal sacrifice turned her uncle into a greatly respected hero among their people.

Though Spotted Tail missed the Great Teton Council at Bear Butte in the Black Hills in 1857, being at the time a "guest" of the U.S. Government at Leavenworth, it is likely the rest of his clan, including Black Shawl and her family, were there for this epochal event. She was almost thirteen years old. It is known that the teenage Crazy Horse was there, and even then, his unusual personality stood out, which would have Marie Sandoz posthumously label him "the strange man of the Oglala." Some have speculated that Black Shawl first saw him at this time and ever since carried a secret torch for him. This is quite possible, as she was an impressionable teenager, faced with an unusually magnetic, commanding personality, and it could also account for the fact that she, most unusual for a Lakota woman in her mid-20s, remained resolutely unmarried, even at the time of being taken to his sickbed, after the No Water shooting in May 1869. The skeins of their lives had come close at various places, such as at the Bluewater Creek, but they probably intersected for the very first time here at Bear Butte, an auspicious locale indeed. However, any feelings at this point were one-sided, as the budding warrior had resounding deeds of valor on his mind rather than women and love. He had a reputation to build, as a peerless fighter and war leader. And, above all, he was still seeking his vision. Women would matter to him, but only in the fullness of time. Meanwhile, Black Shawl quietly nursed her tender feelings for him in private.

Peaceful times prevailed for the Spotted Tail tiyospaye. However, as Ernie LaPoint, the great-grandson of Sitting Bull, put it, "That did not mean the Lakota were at peace, only that the battles that took place were with other tribes. These skirmishes were usually over hunting rights. The fighting was traditional, with more honors granted to the warrior who counted coup, than to one who killed another."

Counting coup involved touching a live enemy in battle, with a coup stick. This showed far greater personal bravery than killing the enemy.

About the middle of 1865 the situation changed, when Spotted Tail led the great raid on the town of Julesburg. After that demonstration, the Army tried to herd his people to a new location, near Fort Kearney. At this fresh intrusion into their lives, Spotted Tail revolted and fled into the North with his people. Black Shawl and her family were almost certainly with his village. However, the Chief did not fight the wasicu and seems to have maintained some lines of communication with them. During that unusually harsh winter, his favorite daughter, Hinzinwin, died. It was said the young girl was in love with a soldier at Fort Laramie and enjoyed sitting on the porch of the administrative building, admiring him on parade. Spotted Tail, therefore, brought her body to Fort Laramie, where a sympathetic Colonel Maynardier had her placed on a traditional Lakota death scaffold for the funerary prayers, a generous gesture honoring the girl's last wishes, which Spotted Tail would not forget. He would never take up arms again. Later, he would move Hinzinwin's bones to his Spotted Tail Agency. Black Shawl was almost certainly present in the camp to mourn her cousin and participate in the ceremonies for her. As a niece of the Chief, it is inconceivable she could be anywhere else.

The Lakotas' Man of Destiny, Crazy Horse (third of that name, which was transferred to him by his father, as had been done by his father before him), was born around 1840, in a small Oglala camp along Rapid Creek in the Black Hills. He was originally called Ca-oha, Among the Trees. His father,

Crazy Horse II, was an Oglala Medicine Man and his mother, Rattling Blanket Woman (who committed suicide after he married the daughters of the widowed Chief Corn, when Crazy Horse was still quite young), was a Miniconjou. Nicknamed Pehin Yuhaha/Jiji or Curly/Light Hair, his name changed to Horse Stands in Sight during his teens, till finally he was transferred the Crazy Horse name by his father in 1861 (when his father renamed himself Waglula or Worm, signifying humility, in the truest Lakota tradition). His half-brother then became Horse Stands in Sight, though by 1870 he was Young Little Hawk, after his own father.

In June 1868, Crazy Horse was awarded the rarest and highest distinction in Lakota warrior society, being made a Shirt-wearer. This was especially remarkable as he was not the son of a chief, the ones expected to receive this honor (nepotism was alive and well, even among the Lakota). Black Shawl was not in the picture then but would certainly have learnt of it in her village.

The first Treaty of Laramie was signed, and broken shortly thereafter, by the settlers and the U.S. Army, driven by the untrammeled greed of the Gold Rush. Despite that, a second Treaty of Laramie was signed in 1868—and broken equally quickly by Custer with his Black Hills Expedition, again lusting for gold. Almost 1000 treaties were signed by the Natives over the years, and every single one was unilaterally broken by the U.S. This particular Treaty was signed by Spotted Tail (who was then rewarded with his own Agency) but not by Red Cloud (who therefore did not get his own Agency till 1871). Red Cloud was still a much-respected warrior and had just concluded two years of "Red Cloud's War," successfully forcing the U.S. Army to abandon all their forts on the Bozeman Trail, which he then promptly burnt to the ground. The U.S. Army would not suffer another such comprehensive defeat till the Vietnam War. The wily, jealous politician in Red Cloud would surface only years later.

BIGHORN TO BETRAYAL

The dust settled on the Great Plains, and life returned to an even tenor for a few years. The seasons turned, the buffalo were still adequate to sustain the people, the Army was mercifully less intrusive. The Lakota lived their lives with a measure of normalcy—without the whisper of a suspicion of what lay just over the horizon, events that would end their largely idyllic existence forever. The inescapable footfall of Destiny, yet indiscernible.

Within this peaceful cocoon, in late May 1869 the calm of the Lakota camps was suddenly shattered, and it would cast a very long shadow over the future. Black Buffalo Woman had decided to leave her alcoholic, abusive husband, and join Crazy Horse at his camp for a late spring hunt in the Slim Buttes area. Her uncle, Black Bear, and his family would be there too. It is every Lakota woman's right to leave her husband for another, if she so chooses, by simply putting his moccasins outside her tipi (the tipi itself always belonged to the woman), and Lakota warriors considered it beneath their dignity to make a fuss over it. However, No Water was cut from a different buckskin and became insanely jealous on his return from another drunken trip with the Laramie Loafers, who habitually hung around the Fort, begging handouts. This was not so much because of his wife leaving him, as it was because of the person she chose to go to. Following the tracks of the hunting party, he located their camp, burst into the communal tipi and shot at Crazy Horse. He was too nervous and scared to take the time to aim carefully. Thanks to Touch the Cloud's quick reaction, his pistol was deflected slightly and the shot only injured the great Shirt-wearer's jaw. The bullet would, however, leave a permanent scar, about which he would be very sensitive all his life, always covering it with his lightning wakinyan paint.

The next day, Spotted Tail arrived with his healer niece, Black Shawl, to care for the wounded man, and this she would do with the dedication and delicacy that could only come from a heart brimming with love for him, as the Edward Clown family confirms. She was probably 22 or 23 years old, the same age as Black Buffalo Woman, and said to be around 5'3", plain of face but with a very good heart. She always wore a black shawl.

Unable to open his mouth due to the damage to his jaw, she handfed him soup through a hollow willow stick and gently rubbed bear fat on the affected area as frequently as possible, while using her considerable knowledge of herbs to reduce his pain. The effects of the care were not long in manifesting themselves, as the warrior rapidly recovered under Black Shawl's ministrations. Deeply touched by her obvious love, despite what he considered his ugly disfigurement he married Black Shawl in June 1870 (according to his closest friend, He Dog, her brother, Red Feather, and the historian Riley), in the Powder River area. Bray claims her parents had presented her, as a potential wife, in 1868, and it had been agreed. However, even Bray admits that Bordeaux, on whom he based this statement, had no evidence beyond "anonymous oral sources" to support his story, and it would have been completely contrary to Crazy Horse's nature to have an affair with Black Buffalo Woman while committed to marrying Black Shawl. Bray concludes, rather lamely, that Bordeaux had "good connections." In the event, she was to be his only wife, ever.

The healing took time and effort, but before too long he was strong enough to resume much of his accustomed activity. Shortly after his marriage, his beloved younger half-brother, Little Hawk, was killed on a war party south of the Platte River. Hearing of this, Crazy Horse immediately set out to recover his body, uncaring that it was 150 miles deep in hostile territory. As would become usual, only Black Shawl accompanied him, despite the considerable danger. Together they located the body and put him on a traditional scaffold to mourn him for nine days. As was customary, Little Hawk's warhorse was sacrificed to accompany him to the other side. During this time, he scoured the hills for miners and killed them without mercy to avenge the death of his kola. Remarkably, no enemy ever came near them, and they eventually journeyed uneventfully back to their own camp. It was clear that, even this early, a strong bond was already being forged between husband and wife.

This is further illustrated by a small domestic incident in the late summer of, probably, 1870, after he had recovered fully and they were married. Crazy Horse had just raided for horses near Fort Laramie. Among the horses were two mares of "Big Bat" Baptiste Pourier, a well-liked man, married to his cousin, Fast Thunder. Pourier came to Crazy Horse to request their return, and he immediately asked Black Shawl to give them to him. A husband's instruction to his wife was usually beyond question in Lakota society, but Black Shawl refused. It is said it took a lot of gentle cajoling by the fierce war chief to finally persuade his wife to return Big Bat's horses. Such obviously was the depth of their relationship. Oral tradition has it that if anyone wanted to find Crazy Horse, it could only be through Black Shawl. She could always find him.

During 1870, his younger half-sister, Shell Blanket, married a man who worked at Fort Bennett, where years later Waglula would covertly draw rations as Kills at Night. The family did not like him, and they were proven right as he eventually abandoned her.

By now, Black Shawl was pregnant, and during this time the couple noticed that his little half-brother, Makah, had befriended a dog that was half wolf. It became utterly devoted to him, following him everywhere, earning Makah the nickname "Wolf." Later, it would become his official identity.

In the spring of 1871, while still in their winter camp at Oglala, near the Black Hills, a daughter was born to Black Shawl and Crazy Horse. He had wanted her to be born in the same place as his grandfather, Walks With Sacred Buffalo. Black Shawl was helped with the delivery by Waglula's wives, Iron Between Horns, Kills Enemy, Red Leggins and, of course, by Good Looking Woman, as well as Crazy Horse's beloved aunt, They Are Afraid of Her. Black Shawl gifted Good Looking Woman her favorite black shawl in gratitude, and she would always treasure it. The other, fearless aunt was honored by having the baby named after her.

The couple doted on little Kokipapi. According to Ernie LaPointe, "In the Lakota language, children are called Wakayaja or Wakan Icaga, meaning 'something sacred is growing.' The Lakota nurtured and took special care of children." Crazy Horse proclaimed her name to the four directions—

Kokipapi, They Are Afraid of Her—wanting her to be a strong, independent, free-spirited, powerful woman like his greatly admired spiritual mother, whom she was named for, always proud to be a Lakota. It was a heartwarming sight to see the great warrior, the terrifying nemesis of all his enemies, white and red, turn to putty in the little, chubby hands of his baby daughter. He spent hours playing with her and cradling her, to the astonishment and wonder of their entire camp. The baby's umbilical cord was put into a buffalo-hide pouch shaped like a turtle, and Crazy Horse always carried it with him. These were days of great contentment for Black Shawl, ones she could only pray would never end.

Fate has ever been a capricious mistress. In the fall of 1873 (the Edward Clown family confirms), when she was just three years old, while Crazy Horse was away on a hunt in his favorite Powder River Valley, his precious daughter passed to the other side. She probably had cholera, a hitherto unknown European disease, against which the Lakota Medicine Men had no defense. Black Shawl would never have another child. On his return, the devastated Crazy Horse immediately set off to locate the scaffold on which her tiny body lay. As Marshall states, "He found her scaffold at the top of a little hill overlooking a small valley north of the Big Horn River." He cared nothing that the location was dangerously close to the territory of his old enemies, the Crows. Black Shawl was in no condition to accompany him on this occasion. He spent three days cradling her little body on the scaffold, mourning deeply, oblivious to the world. Only after the cutting edge of his grief had been blunted a little did he put the pouch with her umbilical cord into her grave and trudge back to camp, to console his equally distraught wife. Tragedy always edged their happiness.

The Edward Clown family disputes this narrative and states that her body was in the camp when Crazy Horse returned. This is obviously more credible, though Marshall's makes for a story more illustrative of his character.

An incident not long after they lost their cherished daughter, narrated by Joseph Marshall III, illustrates the depth of feeling in their relationship: "The gashes across Black Shawl's forearms had not yet scarred. She would always mourn, as he would. She was coughing less and had more of an appetite. She knew that he was preparing to leave again. Black Shawl fixed a meal for him. Sometime after they had eaten, he took her hairbrush and gently brushed her hair, though it was not as long as it once was. In mourning for their daughter, she had cut it to her shoulders. She accepted the gesture in the same spirit that it was given. From his paint bag, he prepared a little mixture, and, with the tip of his finger, colored the part down the middle of her head. He had painted it red. Tomorrow, after he had gone, she would walk among the people and they would see the coloring and know that she was a woman greatly loved. But for the coming night, they would hold off tomorrow and sleep beneath the soft, comforting buffalo robe. They would hold each other close, then she would prepare the dried meat he would need to take along." His story has a ring of authenticity.

Life continued to the even beat of routine for a while in their roving camp as they travelled around the Powder River and Black Hills areas, hunting, camping, celebrating, mourning, praying—the very stuff of everyday lives. Sometime in 1875, while in camp on the Powder, Black Shawl and Crazy Horse celebrated the marriage of his half-brother, James Bear Pipe, the son of Waglula and Red Leggins, to Comes Home Hard Times. It would be the last of the good times. The gathering storm was about to burst upon them.

In mid-June 1876, most of the Lakota and a great number of Cheyenne gathered for a big Sun Dance on the Greasy Grass River, presided over by the great seer-warrior and Crazy Horse's companion-in-arms, Chief Sitting Bull. He had donated one hundred painful pieces of his own flesh to propitiate Wakan Tanka and was recovering from the searing ordeal when word reached the massive camp that a large number of wasicu soldiers, under General George "Three Stars" Crook, were advancing along the Rosebud Valley, toward them, while Lt. Colonel Custer's 7th Cavalry was heading straight for the Little Bighorn. Crazy Horse immediately gathered the warriors and rode overnight to meet Crook. Despite being outnumbered and vastly outgunned by the soldiers and having ridden hard all night to get there, he went into the attack immediately, taking Crook by surprise.

The battle, spread over a three-mile front, lasted about six hours, at the end of which General Crook was forced to withdraw. Harried by the warriors, he was compelled to continue his hasty retreat and would eventually end up all the way back at Fort Fetterman. As Ernie LaPointe, the great-grandson of Sitting Bull, recounts, "The Army troops had expended 25,000 rounds of ammunition to kill a total of twenty Lakota and Cheyenne warriors. The soldiers, on the other hand, had ninety casualties." It is likely this humiliating defeat rankled deeply, and even an otherwise enlightened and insightful man like Crook could not but bear a big grudge against Crazy Horse in his later dealings with him. His retreat also indirectly contributed to Custer's debacle, as he was unable to support him in the critical battle ahead.

The Lakota knew the Rosebud as the Red Flower River, and Black Shawl would have been happy, if unsurprised, to have Crazy Horse back, unharmed, after the battle. His vision had promised that no bullet would ever kill him, and that mystic promise was always a great reassurance for her. The Lakota were deeply spiritual, and it would appear Nature shared the bond.

A week later, Black Shawl watched her husband help win the greatest victory of the Lakota and Cheyenne over the hated soldiers, on the portentous grassy knolls opposite their camp on the Greasy Grass River. While the massive camp celebrated wildly, the senior chiefs understood only too well that this would be their swansong, their end of days.

Once again, no bullet touched her husband. But only Black Shawl remembered, with dread, that the same prophesy also promised if he ever lived near soldiers he would die.

True to his word as a Lakota warrior, when Crazy Horse laid down his arms at Fort Robinson the following year (interestingly, he handed them to the civilian representative of the Department of the Interior, rather than to First Lt. William "Philo" Clark; symbolically, the undefeated warrior never surrendered to the U.S. Army), he never took them up ever again. Even when Crook later tried to force him to fight the rebel Nez Pierce of Chief Joseph, he protested strongly, as he considered it a breach of his promise not to fight again. The wasicu simply did not understand the value of his given word. After all, they had repeatedly demonstrated that their own oral or written words rarely carried much weight.

Fort Robinson, which was established in 1874 primarily to guard the Red Cloud Agency, would remain in military use till 1948, and even serve as a POW camp in World War II. Today, it is a tourist destination—a picnic spot for the oblivious, a place of solemn homage for those who revere the memory of Crazy Horse. All who knew him knew he would always honor his promise. However, the wasicu could not comprehend the code of honor that drove Lakota warriors, having little themselves. They were, after all, mercenaries, fighting for money. Well aware of this and maddened by the awe and respect the young Chief inspired in friend and foe alike, Red Cloud worked to poison the minds of General Crook and Lt. Clark, subtly sowing fear and suspicion in even ordinary soldiers. Sadly, in this devious effort he was aided by an also jealous Spotted Tail, Crazy Horse's own uncle. While the former feared being ousted as the de facto Chief of all the Lakota (he was nominated Chief by the Army, never by his own people), the latter feared Crazy Horse would disrupt the peaceful status quo of his dealings with the wasicu, which he had worked hard to achieve.

Meanwhile, the subject of their plot's only focus was his wife's health. He watched her prosper under Dr. McGillycuddy's care with joy and relief. Sadly, as ever, their happiness was edged with tragedy and Black Shawl was terrified of his vision, having finally failed to dissuade him from coming in to Fort Robinson. She strove to pull him back, fearing for his life while he strove to go in, fearing for hers. Black Shawl instinctively knew it was the end of Lakol Wichohan, their Lakota way of life. Over a century later, Mary Brave Bird articulated the sentiment in her "Ohitika Woman": "I am tired of being dominated by an alien and hostile culture. I am tired of the pressure to adapt to the white men's ideas."

Mid-1877 saw a last joyous occasion for the family, as Black Shawl, Crazy Horse and their family celebrated the wedding of his half-brother, Leo Combing, son of Waglula and the fecund Red Leggins, to Comes After Her. At this time, Black Shawl was still fairly ill and Iron Cedar, his niece, lived with them to look after her. However, by August tensions were rising significantly and she was sent back to the Northern Camp at the Spotted Tail Agency for safety.

Sensing an opportunity to position a spy in his tipi, the U.S. Army, with the enthusiastic collaboration of her father, offered him the half-breed teenaged Ellen "Nellie" Larrabee. Black Shawl, supremely confident in his love for her, offered no objection and he saw Nellie as someone who could care for his wife. Bray claims they fell in love and only Victoria Conroy claims they were "married," but both claims are unsubstantiated and highly improbable. The Army hoped she would pry his "secrets" out through pillow-talk, and this proved just how little they understood the legendary war chief.

The situation at Fort Robinson continued to deteriorate rapidly and, fearing major trouble with the soldiers, egged on by the wily Red Cloud, on September 4, 1877, Crazy Horse took his wife to the village of his ever-loyal cousin, Touch the Clouds, in the Northern Camp at the Spotted Tail Agency for her safety and also because there was a Medicine Man there whom he trusted implicitly. This was most likely his old friend and hunka, Horn Chips. As Marshall recounts, "He and Black Shawl spent the night in the lodge of Touch the Clouds. She sat up at every noise, to his quiet assurances that young men were positioned all around, outside, to prevent trouble." But unknown to them, while Crazy Horse had gone to catch his and Black Shawl's horses, his old comrade-in-arms-turned-traitor, Little Big Man, had hurried to the Army to inform on his movements.

The sympathetic Agent at Camp Sheridan, Jesse Lee, persuaded him to return to Fort Robinson, offering his own personal promise of protection (which, he would realize only later, with great remorse, he could not live up to, despite his best intentions). Crazy Horse left Black Shawl behind, probably in the care of Waglula's wives or Touch the Cloud's family, and was accompanied back to Fort Robinson by Touch the Clouds himself, who suspected all may not turn out as the Agent had promised. After all, Red Cloud with, as it would turn out, the active connivance of General Crook, was plotting to kill him or have him exiled to a living death in the Dry Tortugas, a disease-ridden swamp in Florida that was anything but dry. His half-brothers, Leo Combing and James Bear Pipe, accompanied him and Touch the Clouds to Jesse Lee, but curiously there is no record of the brothers journeying by his side to Fort Robinson. It is likely Crazy Horse had charged them with protecting Black Shawl, with Touch the Clouds being away.

On his return to Fort Robinson in the evening of September 5, he was lured toward the Fort jail, without realizing what it really was. On his way there, he passed Dr. McGillycuddy and gave him a friendly nod. At the door, he finally saw he was entering a jail and not guest accommodation for the night as promised, and broke free to race outside. In the yard, Little Big Man, his friend and comrade of many battles with the wasicu, restrained him, enabling the guard, Private William Gentles, to fatally bayonet him. The perfidious Little Big Man had fulfilled the prophesy, that he would be restrained by his own people and killed while in proximity to soldiers.

It has been suggested that Gentles panicked and struck him accidentally, but this is not credible as he was a veteran of many years, having fought extensively, not the sort of person to panic and mishandle a bayonet. Clearly, he had orders to kill Crazy Horse whenever an opportunity arose, and the infamous Little Big Man was part of the plot. The Army and the Government were only too anxious to be rid of this embarrassment, whom they had never been able to subdue and who had not only defeated Crook himself, twice, but wiped out their darling Custer. Brian Pohanka of *Time/Life Books* summed it up eloquently: "…the Army felt the whole business was mismanaged—even that intelligent officer, Philo Clark, seems to have been misled by his pro-Red Cloud informants. Crook also failed to step in and mediate the crisis as was his responsibility. The death of Crazy Horse was, in short, a tragedy just as Wounded Knee was, moreover it was a 'tragedy' in the Shakespearean sense as well, for a great man was slain by a lesser man. There is a sad sense of inevitability about the whole episode." That day, the U.S. Army covered itself in infamy—once again.

After protracted arguments with the Fort Commandant, forcing even American Horse to step up and demand dignity for a fallen chief who should not be put into a jail, amidst the mounting anger of his people, Dr. McGillycuddy had him moved into the Adjutant's office nearby to tend to him. He was accompanied by Touch the Clouds, and Waglula arrived shortly thereafter. On their way, Waglula and Red Leggins had passed He Dog, heading away from the Fort, and he confirmed Crazy Horse was injured but not dead yet (it is an enduring puzzle why He Dog, one of his closest and oldest friends, did not stay with him at the end). The Doctor knew the wound was fatal and could only try to lessen his pain. The great man's life slowly ebbed with the fading starlight as Crazy Horse finally travelled to the other side. It was the end of an epoch of giants. Only Ambrose claims Black Shawl and They Are Afraid of Her were at Fort Robinson at the time of the assassination and that they both lived at Pine Ridge thereafter, but these claims are unsubstantiated and clearly incorrect.

As Little Big Man and Private Gentles quickly went into hiding (they would eventually leave the area, and the former probably even change his name, to try and hide his infamy), in the dawn light Crazy Horse's old father and Touch the Clouds took his body in an Army ambulance back to his bereft

Lone Horn Camp. Word of the treachery having quickly reached the Northern Camp at Spotted Tail Agency, just 45 miles away, the ailing Black Shawl, accompanied by the redoubtable They Are Afraid of Her, rushed to his camp. But by then, they could only weep over his body—Black Shawl's apprehensions, based on his vision, had been fully, nightmarishly realized.

Placing his body gently on a travois, they headed, with leaden steps, to Camp Sheridan, near the Spotted Tail Agency. As Bray described it, "Taking up the reins, Worm and his wife walked toward the camp entrance. Behind the travois walked Black Shawl, eyes downcast on the bundle." The love of her life was gone, and a great tremulous blankness stretched before her. Accompanying her were Iron Cedar and They Are Afraid of Her. According to Bray, "Crazy Horse's hunka brother, Horn Chips, accompanied the little group." On September 8, his body was placed on a death scaffold near Camp Sheridan by the guilt-ridden Lt. Jesse Lee, and Black Shawl mourned at its foot. On the 12th, a wooden barricade would be erected around it for protection. Records surviving at the National Archives in Kansas City, Missouri, show that on September 16, Waglula (recorded as "Crazy Horse's Father") and his family, including Black Shawl, officially transferred from the treacherous Red Cloud Agency to the Spotted Tail Agency. The former, for now, was as much enemy territory as the land of their old foes, the Crows.

In October 1877, the Whetstone Agency, which had been founded under the second Treaty of Laramie in 1868, was moved from its location on White Clay Creek in Nebraska to the old Ponca Agency near Yankton, on the Missouri River. In 1874 it had been renamed the Spotted Tail Agency and Camp Sheridan built near it, on Beaver Creek, northeast of Hayes Springs, operating till it was abandoned in 1881. The Agency would move yet again in 1878 to Rosebud and be renamed the Rosebud Reservation.

During the move to the old Ponca Agency, an interesting and credible event took place, according to Victoria Conroy. She was the daughter of Lena, who was married to Standing Bear, the son of Big Woman (sister of Waglula) and One Horse. She was eleven years old at the time of her cousin's assassination. In a letter dictated on December 18, 1934, she stated that on the march to the old Ponca Agency, Waglula secretly substituted his son's covered body on the travois with the carcass of a deer. During the move, he stealthily drifted away from the procession and buried his son, in secret, possibly near Pepper Creek, southwest of Manderson, on the Pine Ridge Reservation. Much later, on the return trek, he and Horn Chips surreptitiously reburied him at an unknown location, thought to be somewhere between Porcupine and Wounded Knee Creek. Black Shawl, according to Victoria, was not told the location in the belief that she could remarry someday and could reveal it. In the event she never did remarry, as confirmed by her brother Red Feather, as well as Census records at the National Archives. Thomas Kine (father of Ida Killer) met her at Oglala, South Dakota, shortly before her death, and she confirmed she did not know where Crazy Horse was buried. The humble warrior, whose indefatigable defence of his people and their way of life made him so much larger than life, rests in peace forever, with no living person today aware of his location.

It is at this point in the narrative that Black Shawl fades into the mists of history, seemingly without a trace. This is hardly surprising, as all historians have overlooked her story in the towering shadow of Crazy Horse's epic saga. This is unfortunate, particularly considering the influence she had on him and how their relationship moulded the course of events, directly and indirectly.

Looking out of my study, a world away, in the Sultanate of Oman, I mulled this, gazing at a rare, fading photograph of the unassuming, gentle person, trying hard to plumb the depths of her soul. Historical oblivion, for such as she, seemed deeply unfair and unjust. And thus began the hunt for Crazy Horse's women. It would take almost three years to piece her story together, based on documentary evidence culled from the National Archives over two extended visits, oral family histories of the Lakota, familial travels, logical deductions from various external factors, and even the occasional throwaway observations of major historians, for whom she was insignificant, as she was not their principal focus of interest, but which often proved invaluable in directing my own search for the lost ladies of the Lakota.

FORT ROBINSON TO FORT BENNETT

The years were not kind to Black Shawl and her husband's relatives. They were forced into hiding, as a vengeful Government and Army systematically hunted members of their family, and Red Cloud helped with information whenever he found any leads to them. It was not enough to assassinate Crazy Horse; it was necessary to wipe out all traces of him and his legacy. The tenacity of the Government's search and its sheer vindictiveness can be gauged from an incident that took place as late as January 1918, over forty years after Crazy Horse's murder, when Makah (Earth), also known as Peter Wolf, was overheard admitting to being a half-brother of Crazy Horse, in a rare, unguarded moment at Cherry Creek. On the drive back from the town to his home, he was waylaid near Rudy Creek and murdered by bounty hunters who had overheard him.

There were, however, enough Lakota who remembered the glory days and the great lengths Crazy Horse had gone to, to protect and provide for even the weakest and most helpless of his people. Despite the schism in the Lakota tiyospaye, created by Red Cloud and Spotted Tail, his people and even many from the other bands remained staunchly loyal to the memory of the late Chief and helped hide the family from prying eyes. Even today, when one could be forgiven for believing the danger passed, the descendants of Waglula are extremely guarded, reticent and wary. Generational trauma has reconfigured their very DNA. It is only in the last few years that Waglula's descendants, the Clown family, have finally shared some of their story with the writer and filmmaker William Matson. Indeed, even my friend, the full-blood Vernell White Thunder, who lives on the Pine Ridge Reservation and has a network of relatives across the other two Lakota reservations as well, would only console me, "Good luck on your blind trail."

By the December of 1877, Black Shawl had disappeared from even the Spotted Tail Agency. As the most vulnerable of his relatives, she would have been especially carefully guarded by those around Waglula, and even more so by Touch the Clouds, who stood rock-solid with his cousin to the very end. In the Census of that month, "Crazy Horse's Father" had just two women with him, obviously his wives, Iron Between Horns and Red Leggins. This is further substantiated by a stray annotation in the May 1878 Census records: "Crazy Horse's wife left Spotted Tail Agency without authorization for parts unknown," along with a group, for cover and protection, before December 1877.

As the tentacles of their enemies began to probe deeper and deeper into the Spotted Tail Agency, Black Shawl was smuggled across to the Cheyenne River Agency, protected by well-wishers, possibly including the family of Waglula's old friend Kills At Night, whose name he would briefly assume later, according to the Edward Clown Family, as cover to confuse those on his tracks. As the Edward Clown family states, "Black Shawl had moved north with our family and now lived in the same tipi as They Are Afraid of Her. They stayed together in our family camp." In 1883, they were living in a small stucco cabin at Thunder Butte, in present-day South Dakota, about ninety miles north of Cherry Creek, near which Julia Iron Cedar moved after she married Amos Clown. The Cheyenne River Lakota were distanced from the two plotters, Red Cloud and Spotted Tail, and revered Crazy Horse. Having got Black Shawl to safety, the other family members bided their time.

However, the highly toxic atmosphere did not improve, and a few months later, in 1878, Waglula and Touch the Clouds also moved their camps to present-day Cherry Creek, on the Cheyenne River Reservation, where they were probably joined by Black Shawl and They Are Afraid of Her. Understandably, they took care not to leave a paper trail of official transfer requests. As a result, "Crazy Horse's Father" continued to appear on the Spotted Tail Census till 1880, but thereafter there is no trace of even a single member of Waglula's family there. In every Cheyenne River Census, the Waglula/Breast of Female family featured directly after the listing for the

Touch the Clouds family, indicating they lived next to each other, in the same village, as also did Peter Wolf's family, Combing's and Iron Cedar's. After the death of Touch the Clouds, in 1905, his son, Paul Touch the Clouds, continued to draw rations at Cherry Creek. Curiously, the Red Horse family (of my "Red Herring" fame), too, seem to have been their neighbors all along.

After 1880, "Crazy Horse's Father" finally vanishes from the Census and, from 1881 to 1886, seems to have lived at Cheyenne River under the name of his friend Kills at Night, who had moved to join his son at the Red Cloud Agency, leaving him his Cheyenne River Ration Ticket. Thereafter, he is documented at Cheyenne River as Breast of Female (Ticket #359) till his death in 1901. His last wife, Red Leggins, outlived him by four years, passing to the other side in 1905. He drew rations from Fort Bennett (the outpost built in 1870 and abandoned just 21 years later, now submerged under the Oahe Reservoir), under that name. This would not have been too difficult, as many Lakota did not register their true names in the Census or even Ration Tickets, for fear of persecution. Their deaths, too, were often unreported, and this would certainly be true of the Crazy Horse family. A case in point is They Are Afraid of Her, for whom there are simply no extant records of any sort at any of the three reservations. The absence of records for such a prominent family, against well-documented ones for insignificant ones, also points to the fact that they were forced into hiding. This would change only very slowly, over succeeding generations, till we find, in March 1922, allotments of 160 acres each, in Township #16 of Whitehorse, Cheyenne River Reservation, recorded for Peter Clown, Mollie Clown and Lillie Clown.

After his friend's death in 1886, it became dangerous to continue using his name and so he assumed the name of Tatanka Makuhu, the name of his brother-in-law, Hump (Buffalo Breastbone, which seems to have been, mystifyingly, mistranslated by contemporary recorders as Breast of Female or Woman's Breast), living with his surviving wife, Red Leggins, the other, Iron Between Horns, having passed to the other side in 1880, the cause of her death unspecified. His use of the Breast of Female name was further confirmed by his son, Leo Combing, in his probate testimony in August 1920. They lived quietly near Bear Creek at that time.

Between 1886 and 1899, the Cheyenne River Census records "Breast of Female" living with "Red Legs" and Iron Cedar, her daughter born in

1868. Sloppy clerks in 1886 show both Makuhu's and Red Legs' ages incorrectly, as 61 years, but Iron Cedar is correctly recorded as eighteen years old. Iron Cedar, having married, moved out of this household to her own tipi by the 1900 Census, a year before her father's death. Breast of Female appears in the June 1901 Census, aged 76 years, but in 1902 Red Legs is alone. Makuhu passed to his ancestors on September 7, 1901, and was buried in Bear Creek. William Garnett claimed he died at the Rosebud Reservation but this is incorrect, as Waglula was in hiding at the time. Finally, the aged and prolific Red Legs is missing in the 1905 Census, having finally passed to her rest.

Black Shawl continued to live "under the radar." She never changed her name, and contrary to expectations she never remarried, remaining close to the family of her husband. Around this time, Leo Combing had another son, sparking a flicker of joy and celebration in the hunted family. Sadly, the baby died soon after, piling more grief on them, coming as it did on the heels of Iron Between Horns' death.

In 1882, Leo Combing had another son, and Black Shawl assisted at the birth or, at the very least, was present for the celebrations. The Cheyenne River Reservation was proving to be a reasonably safe haven for the fugitives.

In 1890, Crazy Horse's half-brother, Makah/Peter Wolf (a son of Waglula and the prolific Red Leggins), quietly married Margaret Makes the Squeal, somewhere around Bridger or Cherry Creek, an event that Black Shawl would definitely have attended, probably travelling from Pine Ridge to do so. Shortly thereafter, Crazy Horse's half-sister, Iron Cedar, married Amos Clown and Black Shawl could not possibly have been missing from that celebration either, having always been close to her emotionally.

That may have been the last time she could travel, as the Government restricted all Lakota movements thereafter, following the Wounded Knee Massacre. His half-brother, Peter Wolf, had a son, John, the same year, and Julia Iron Cedar had a son, Moses/Bear with Horns, in 1891, whose resemblance to Crazy Horse was said to be uncanny. After he was killed in World War I, Julia would become the first Gold Star mother in South Dakota. The Government was still apprehensive of the Crazy Horse legacy but realized it could not go after the mother of a war hero. In 1892, his other half-brother, James Bear Pipe, passed to the other side. It is unlikely that Black Shawl was there to assist with the ceremonies, as she was ageing by then, and because of the Government restrictions on their travel, even between Reservations.

Black Shawl lived with They Are Afraid of Her till at least 1886 but was no longer with her when she died in 1889. She was buried on the Owl (Moreau) River, between Thunder Butte and Green Grass, as per the Edward Clown family. They claim Black Shawl then moved to an aunt on the Rosebud Reservation, where she died and was buried in Mission, South Dakota. This is unlikely, as census documents show her living with her mother, Red Elk, at the Pine Ridge Reservation from 1887. This could be the result of intentional misdirection by a traumatized family to protect her resting place or confusion over the exact details for a relatively minor member in a male-dominated society. Either way, continued oblivion is simply unfair to the memory of this gentle soul.

The respected historian Kingsley Bray confirms she moved to White Clay Creek, in the Pine Ridge Reservation, to care for her ageing, widowed mother, Red Elk, who was living alone (though elsewhere he contradicts this by stating she remained with Waglula's family which, I believe, she did a couple of years after her mother passed). This is likely the only reason that could compel Black Shawl to leave her longtime tipi-mate and protector, They Are Afraid of Her, at least two years before the latter passed. Her mother was probably seriously ailing at this time and needed her support, whereas the indefatigable They Are Afraid of Her continued to be robust. The White Clay Census of 1887 records her name as "Her Black Blanket" (43 years in 1887, she becomes 42 years the following year, as "Her Blanket," reverting to "Her Black Blanket" in 1890 and the enumerators finally settling on "Black Shawl" from 1892 onwards, though by the 1900 Census she is 47 years old, according to them), living with Red Elk (seventy years in 1898, she was recorded as 67 years in 1890). The 1892 and 1893 records even show a Makes Alive (probably an eighteen-year-old nephew, the son of Black Shawl's sister, Makes Alive) living with them, though why he did so at that stage of his life and for such a short period will never be known. They may have lived near the Holy Rosary Mission, with the Oglala Spleen/Melt band of Chief Yellow Bear.

According to this postulation, Black Shawl lived with her mother for more than a decade, till she passed in 1898. For some unknown reason, during the census in 1895, Red Elk is missing, though Black Shawl is present, with a Ticket #359. The 1899 White Clay Census finds Black Shawl living alone, marked as Head of Household, evidence that Red Elk had passed in the preceding year. By then, it can be assumed that the enmity of the now-blind Red Cloud had become ineffective, and there were more than enough admirers of Crazy Horse at the Pine Ridge Reservation to assure her safety.

After the Wounded Knee Massacre on December 29, 1890, the Government severely restricted all travel for the Lakota, even between Reservations, and stepped up the hunt for Crazy Horse's male relatives. The same year, the Red Cloud Agency was renamed Pine Ridge Reservation, and the Spotted Tail Agency split into the Cheyenne River Reservation, Standing Rock Reservation and Rosebud Reservation. The acreage of all areas, as well as rations, were cut sharply. This split may possibly explain some of the confusion between the Rosebud Reservation and Cheyenne River Reservation in some historical accounts.

Oral family history confirms she had moved back to her husband's family, on the Cheyenne River Reservation, after her mother passed to her ancestors. The two single women, Black Shawl and They Are Afraid of Her, had always been close and had formed a strong mutual support team. When They Are Afraid of Her died in 1889 and Waglula in 1901, Black Shawl was truly alone. It is likely that around 1902 or so, Black Shawl moved to the Cherry Creek area, to the tiyospaye of Touch the Clouds and his descendants, and stayed in that area till her death. Curiously, the Government-harried family of her husband's dear friend, Sitting Bull, was also later forced to hide out fairly close to this location, in the Badlands of the Dakotas.

Black Shawl is briefly missing from the Censuses of 1912 and 1922, but that is likely due to clerical oversight, as was all too common at the time. However, from 1900 onwards it is unclear if we are seeing Crazy Horse's Black Shawl or another (my Red Herring). Curiously, her brother, Red Feather, and his family appear to have continued on at the renamed Rosebud Reservation and show up in its Register of Indian Families till at least 1925. While many of these conclusions are necessarily suppositions, they make logical sense, based on oral family histories, as well as available documentary data, and are thus very likely to be accurate.

By the time Red Leggins passed, the only surviving siblings of Crazy Horse were Combing, Makah and Iron Cedar. Makah was murdered on January 19, 1918; Leo Combing passed on November 3, 1932; and Julia Iron Cedar joined her ancestors on July 10, 1936, dying of heat stroke, drawing down the curtain on the Crazy Horse generation with a certain finality.

Eventually, likely at the ripe old age of eighty years—a remarkable achievement, especially considering her history of ill health, till the intervention of Dr. McGillycuddy—Black Shawl joined her husband. There are four versions of the year and place she died.

Her brother, Red Feather, always averred she died of the flu in Pine Ridge in 1927 but may have confused the location or, more likely, used this as a diversionary tactic to protect her grave, though the cause of death could very well have been the flu. We will never know for sure, since no Death Records exist for her there.

There does exist a full Death Certificate and record in various Births and Deaths Registers of a Black Shawl who passed in Cherry Creek on November 1, 1925, also aged eighty years, and was buried in the Congregational Cemetery at Bridger. Her age and all the other details match "our" Black Shawl. The difficulty is with the date of death. Where her own brother puts it at 1927, and I have used that date in her family tree, this record clearly states she died on November 1, 1925, at eighty years of age. An even bigger puzzle, though, is that her Ticket #309 in the Death Registers (but not on the Death Certificate) belonged to Red Horse's Black Shawl. While there is no way to know definitively, the weight of evidence seems to favor this version of her death.

The Edward Clown family claims she died in 1907, at the age of 68 years, at the Rosebud Reservation, where she had relatives. They certainly should know, but this date is clearly incorrect, as her age does not add up since she was born most likely in 1845 or 1846 and this would push that year back to 1841 or 1842, making her almost as old as her husband, which we know for certain was not the case. Moreover, the location, too, does not tally with the Census documents, which prove she was at Pine Ridge. Ambrose is furthest out, claiming she died in 1930, at the then very improbable age of 85 years. In the June 1895 Census of the Pine Ridge Reservation, there is a Black Shawl, living alone, aged 85 years, which could have misled some researchers. However, since she was 85 years old in 1895, she certainly could not have been "our" Black Shawl. With her passing, the contemporaries of Crazy Horse gently faded to dust, without leaving any voice for the unborn generations.

There is no word in Lakota for goodbye. What is said, instead, means "See you again" –Toksha Akhay.

Thus ended the direct line of Crazy Horse.
Unless…

BLACK
BUFFALO
WOMAN

(TATANKA SAPE WIN)

TIMELINE FOR BLACK BUFFALO WOMAN

1841	Chief Bull Bear killing by Red Cloud
1846	Black Buffalo Woman born
Sep 1851	Horse Creek / Fort Laramie Treaty
Aug 1854	Grattan Fight
Sep 1855	Bluewater Creek Massacre
1857	Met Crazy Horse at Great Teton Council at Bear Butte
1862	Forcibly married to No Water by Red Cloud
1863	First son, Young No Water, born
1865	Second son born
	Crazy Horse made Shirtwearer (Ogle Tanka Un)
1866	Visited Crazy Horse's camp with Red Cloud & No Water
1866 – 1868	Red Cloud's War
1867	Third son born
21-25 May 1869	Shooting of Crazy Horse by No Water
Jun 1870	*Fourth child, light-haired daughter, born*
1871	1st Red Cloud Agency / No Water surrendered
1874	IF Black Crow, fifth son born, Rising Star/Star Comes Out
1875	Great Council held on White River about Black Hills
Early 1876	Crazy Horse and Twins together near Bear Butte.
	No Water & Black Buffalo Woman very likely there too.
	Black Twin died late 1876
25 Jun 1876	Battle of Greasy Grass / Little Bighorn
6 May 1877	Chief Crazy Horse comes into Fort Robinson
5 Sep 1877	ASSASSINATION OF CHIEF CRAZY HORSE
1878	Sixth son born, Winter/North
10 Jul 1936	Ambrose & He Dog claim daughter still alive

CRIME PASSIONNEL

"Crazy Horse, I have come for you!" screamed the incensed No Water as he barreled into the large communal tipi, brandishing a pistol borrowed from an unwary friend. Completely contrary to Lakota tradition, the insanely jealous man had come to try and wrest back his wife, Black Buffalo Woman, who had decided, as the Lakota author Joseph Marshall III confirms, "to followed her heart and left her husband. Lakota women could make such a choice because societal norms allowed it, but in her case a jealous husband did not." She joined Crazy Horse on his spring buffalo hunt, in either the Slim Buttes or Powder River area (sources differ on the location). Her uncle, Black Bear, her cousin and He Dog's brother, Little Shield, and their families were part of the group. She left her children with her mother-in-law, probably indicating an exasperated last-minute decision to leave. This occurred in May or June 1870, say Bordeaux, Larson, and Hinman, based on his conversations with He Dog. However, logical timelines would suggest it was in the spring of 1869.

Spotting Crazy Horse, seated in the place of honor in the circle of friends, family and elders, No Water immediately fired. In a curious foreshadowing of events to come, Little Big Man quickly prevented Crazy Horse from drawing his knife, but Crazy Horse's cousin, Touch the Clouds, sitting near the entrance, swiftly hit No Water's arm and deflected the bullet. It crashed into his jaw instead and exited through his cheek, wounding him grievously but not mortally. Again, his youthful vision proved true, that no bullet would ever kill him.

No Water, having expended his meagre courage, rapidly took to his horse and raced to escape. Touch the Clouds, Standing Elk and others immediately gave chase, determined to kill him for this unforgiveable offence. Desperate, No Water flogged his horse for mile after mile, fleeing for the safety of his cousin Red Cloud's camp. Resting briefly at Nisland, he continued flogging his horse till it eventually dropped dead at the White Earth River. Running the short distance to Red Shirt Table, he commandeered another horse and dashed on, with death dogging his heels. He was barely able to stay ahead of Touch the Clouds but finally sprinted into the sanctuary of Red Cloud's camp.

Edward Star, a present-day direct descendent of No Water, generously shared with me the account of this incident that has come down through his family's oral history tradition, which tells a vastly different story:

"My uncle, Winfred No-Water / Bores A Hole, related the story of a peace medal issued by Ulysses Grant just before the end of the Civil War (1854), which was distributed by Father priest DeSmet to all the leaders in the territory of the Lakota/Dakota/Nakota people. Winfred was called Cahli (Coal) by the tiospaye and he had one of these peace medals that belonged to Crazy Horse. No Water wanted to warn Crazy Horse that those who received these medals were being hunted down and murdered (exterminated) by a detachment of Union soldiers, and so, when he told Crazy Horse, he told No Water to snap the medal from his neck. In doing so, he knocked over a rifle, which went off and it shot Crazy Horse in the face. Stories and rumours, at that time, spread the word that No Water shot Crazy Horse over his wife Black Buffalo Woman. The medal was handed down by No Water generations and Cahli said his dad, Willie, gave him the medal. Cahli had credited groceries from the Howard Reeves store in White Clay, Nebraska, where he took the medal to pay his debt, he received more groceries from the store. It was believed that, later, Reeves took the medal to the museum in Deadwood, South Dakota. Cahli died in the late 1960s."

One of the peculiar fallouts of this incident was that Crazy Horse's hunka and Medicine Man, Horn Chips, was severely harassed by the Bad Faces clan of Red Cloud, for being loyal to Crazy Horse and shortly thereafter left the band for good, moving to the Rosebud Reservation. Even more strangely, the harassment was primarily by Black Twin, who would later often camp with

Crazy Horse and "stayed out" with him when the Red Cloud family surrendered.

The moment she heard his voice, Black Buffalo Woman knew he had come for her. Hearing the shot, she quickly rolled out under the tipi flap at the rear and escaped to her uncle Black Bear's tent for refuge. She would remain hidden there, even after No Water had been chased all the way back to his camp. Meanwhile, Crazy Horse was severely injured and in great pain. Being a hunting camp, there was no one there capable of treating his injury.

Word of such a cataclysmic event traveled fast, as the Lakota feared for the life of their great war leader with very few apparently supporting No Water. When he heard of it, his uncle, Spotted Tail, left for the camp at once with his niece, Black Shawl, a noted healer. Two days after the shooting, Red Cloud, too, arrived to collect his niece from Black Bear. After some discussion, Crazy Horse allowed him to take her back to No Water but only after he had undertaken to personally ensure she would not be ill-treated by him, as she had been in the past. Red Cloud agreed, as he, too, a proud Lakota warrior himself, could not but have considered his kinsman's behavior beneath contempt. However, in a clear sign of his rancor for the young man even then, he demanded that Crazy Horse's Shirt be taken from him and awarded to No Water. The Elders disagreed, but Crazy Horse himself returned the honor shortly thereafter, giving it back to the Elder who had awarded it to him. Despite Red Cloud's active and continued lobbying, that Shirt was permanently retired and never awarded to anyone ever again.

It is unlikely that Black Buffalo Woman and Crazy Horse were ever in contact with each other again, and this dramatic finale closed the chapter on their tumultuous relationship. This was further cemented as he gradually fell in love with Black Shawl and then married her. Unlike many Lakota, including his own uncle, who had five wives and thirty-five children, he never believed in taking more than one wife. Though He Dog once said his friend had "married" Black Buffalo Woman, their one night together on a hunt makes that highly unlikely, and even he later contradicted this by saying Crazy Horse had to return his Shirt because of "adultery." The Edward Clown family, as well as all major historians, agree that there is no evidence of a marriage. Black Shawl would be the only wife he ever had. While Ambrose claimed this incident took place in 1871, after his great mentor, Hump, was killed, it is generally agreed that all available evidence indicates it actually took place earlier, in May 1869. From here, Black Buffalo Woman's footprint in history fades rapidly into utter oblivion.

Though some historians claim her birth year as 1841, the year of Bull Bear's murder by Red Cloud, which permanently divided the Oglala into the Old Smoke and Bull Bear camps, it is much more likely to have been 1846, as the respected Kingsley Bray asserts. She was almost the same age as Black Shawl. Her grandparents were Walks as She Thinks, the mother of Red Cloud, and Lone Man, Waglula's mentor. While her parents are not known definitively, Bray had reason to believe her father was one of Red Cloud's brothers, probably Spider/Tall Hollow Horn, and her mother, a daughter of American Horse, most likely Red Tipi. Among her cousins was Crazy Horse's dearest friend, He Dog.

As Old Smoke's village, of which she was a part, were Laramie Loafers, she, like Black Shawl, must have been in or near the camp during the bloody Grattan Fight in August 1854. However, it was not till the June 1857 Summer Solstice gathering at Bear Butte that she, at almost twelve years of age, was old enough to be aware of Crazy Horse and, most historians as well as the Edward Clown family agree, developed a permanent crush on him. Over the next couple of years, they would see each other in the camps on and off, like ships that pass in the night, and it seems he gradually began to reciprocate her feelings. By all accounts, she was a very beautiful woman.

At this juncture, their story acquires a romantic hue. Ambrose believes he began to actively court her, lining up with other suitors outside her tipi with his courting robe, in the traditional courting manner. Sandoz takes the next event a step further, saying, in 1862, Red Cloud invited Crazy Horse to a hunt and then quietly sent No Water back to camp, feigning a toothache. He then had Black Buffalo Woman married off to No Water (Mni Sni), while Crazy Horse was away. Though there is no evidence of this, it does make for a credibly star-crossed tale of tragic lovers, worthy of Shakespeare. However, there is, as Marshall points out, no doubt that "her family had plans that didn't take the girl's own feelings into consideration."

As there is only one No Water (Mni Sni) in the early census rolls, it is relatively easy to follow him—for as long as his family used that name. He was born of an Oglala father and a Cheyenne mother and was the brother of

Black Twin (Holy Bald Eagle) and White Twin (Holy Buffalo). Ironically, the Twins would always remain on friendly terms with Crazy Horse, frequently camping and hunting together, and White Twin even brought his camp in to Fort Robinson alongside him after the death of Black Twin. Since No Water was often in his brothers' camp, it is very likely that Black Buffalo Woman saw Crazy Horse on these occasions, fueling her love for him. All confirm she was much sought after by the young bucks before her marriage. However, it does seem that her heart was always set on just one, Crazy Horse.

In 1863, Black Buffalo Woman gave birth to her first son, Young No Water. While records of this son's wife and their offspring are missing, we do know he had a grandson, Ivan Star Comes Out, who died in 1937. His grandson, Edward Star, lives on the Pine Ridge Reservation today and teaches at the Oglala Lakota College, a rare instance where a direct line can be traced to one of Crazy Horse's contemporaries. At some point, Young No Water's successors changed their name to Star Comes Out, and eventually just Star.

In 1865 and 1867, Black Buffalo Woman had two more sons, followed by a light-haired daughter in 1870, less than a year after her escapade with Crazy Horse, though there is no trace of these children in the records. This possible child of the great Chief was alive in 1930, as confirmed by He Dog to Hinman, and Ambrose claims she was alive in 1936. Unfortunately, the contemporary Star family is reticent about their relatives and what became of them.

POWDER RIVER TO OBLIVION

In 1865, the same year as Spotted Tail's great raid on Julesburg, Crazy Horse was honored as a Shirt-wearer, and all reports indicate Black Buffalo Woman went out of her way to lionize him and taunt her husband. This understandably inflamed No Water's jealousy, building up to the infamous shooting. It is clear, even from this alone, well evidenced in family oral histories, that she loved Crazy Horse and had married No Water under familial duress. So, Mari Sandoz' narrative of the marriage-by-trickery might just be accurate.

In the summer of 1866, she visited Crazy Horse's camp with Red Cloud, and her feelings were revived. She was about twenty years old. Surprisingly, No Water and she stayed on there, after Red Cloud left, but friction with Crazy Horse began almost immediately because of No Water's alcoholism and the inevitable beatings of his wife that followed his drunken forays. Crazy Horse warned him against this, saying he would encourage her to leave him, as was her Lakota right, if he persisted in his ill treatment of her. No Water simply laughed and ignored his admonishments, probably because he always knew he enjoyed Red Cloud's protection, and the fact that Crazy Horse never lost his regard for the role model of his youth and would not embarrass him.

In his youth, as Marshall confirms, Crazy Horse had courted Black Buffalo Woman and "the grain of hope Light Hair had dared to hold, as he watched the line of suitors at Black Buffalo Woman's lodge, grew into a distinct possibility for the young and daring Crazy Horse." According to the Clown family, Crazy Horse liked her but never courted her, as she was already married to No Water. However, Marshall is referencing a time before her marriage. Being an alcoholic, No Water would frequently go to trading posts to drink. And it was while he was away on one such excursion to the Fort that she finally had enough and decided to leave him for Crazy Horse, joining him on his spring buffalo hunt, shortly after the signing of the second Fort Laramie Treaty by Red Cloud and others.

That Treaty led to the founding of the first "sod" Red Cloud Agency in 1871, a mile west of present-day Henry, Nebraska, on the North Platte River. While Red Cloud was at Fort Laramie finalizing this site, he constantly sought the approval of No Water's brother, Black Twin. So, No Water, Black Buffalo Woman and their children were probably there too. It was strange that Red Cloud sought his advice, especially on something as important as this, as the Twins generally acted in a manner the opposite of everything Red Cloud did. Hence, they stayed out, independent, with Crazy Horse and did not come into his Red Cloud Agency with those relatives. And so, too, very surprisingly, did No Water, at least for a while, though, ever afraid of Crazy Horse and jealous of Black Buffalo Woman's unconcealed admiration for him, he stayed well away from the Hunkpatila camp, as far as humanly possible.

White Twin would eventually join the desperate breakout from the Red Cloud Agency, racing for the hoped-for freedom of Canada, but would die there. Though the Twins stayed together all their lives, Black Twin, always the more measured of the two, died suddenly in 1876; White Twin surrendered with Crazy Horse, as noted in the Crazy Horse Surrender Ledger, and remained near his village till his desperate break for Canada. No Water had already come in, in 1871 probably following Sword's peace mission to the northern bands. In 1874, he is recorded as part of the akicita there and eventually he would be delegated by Red Cloud to oversee the Bad Faces band at the Red Cloud Agency, according to Hyde. This is further evidenced by the 1876 Ration Roll, which shows he drew supplies for about 600 people under him, according to Bray.

Black Buffalo Woman and her children came in with No Water's camp, but that name completely disappears from this point. There is, however, a Black Crow living with a No Water, and it is just possible careless census agents mistranslated her name to Black Crow or Black Cow Woman. If this was indeed Black Buffalo Woman, the 1886 Pine Ridge Census indicates she gave birth to a fifth and sixth son, Rising Star and Winter, in 1874 and 1878. The parents' ages tally within the usual erratic margin of error for those rolls.

By 1886, Young No Water has disappeared from the family tipi as, being 23 years old, he had probably married and moved out. We know he survived his youth, as there is a direct line traceable to him today in Edward Star, his great-great-great-grandson. The same is likely to have happened with the other three children, who would have been 21, 19 and 17 years respectively in 1886. It is, of course, possible that one or more of them died young, as was unfortunately often the case at that time. The only people who could reasonably be expected to have knowledge of this, the Edward Star family, are a little uncertain of details. My correspondence with Edward Star on this score, always responded to with classic Lakota courtesy and good manners, leaves some room for confusion. This is really a huge pity, as a people who lose their history, like their language, lose their very identity. This makes the decision of the Edward Clown family to share their oral family history so wise and wonderful. History is heritage, and the loss of any part of our common human heritage affects the whole.

During 1875, when the great conclave of over 20,000 Lakota was held on the White River to discuss the sale of the sacred Black Hills that the gold-hungry U.S. Government demanded, No Water and Black Buffalo Woman would almost certainly have been present. It is not documented anywhere whether Crazy Horse attended this gathering. The following year, Crazy Horse and Black Twin camped together near Bear Butte. No Water, and therefore Black Buffalo Woman, too, were most likely with Black Twin's village, though it is reasonable to assume she avoided Crazy Horse for fear of her husband. It is also reasonable to assume she was present at the Red Cloud Agency with No Water on that fateful September 5, 1877, though there is no mention of her anywhere in records of any sort. She would have mourned Crazy Horse deeply, in private.

By the 1887 Census, Rising Star has become Star Comes Out and Winter has become North, though the reasons for the changes are unknown. They are in evidence till 1890, after which they vanish. In 1887, however, the most interesting element is that No Water's wife is now Brings Plenty, who is five years older than Black Crow and ten years older than Black Buffalo Woman is likely to have been. So, it is very likely that Black Buffalo Woman/Black Crow left him that year or, more likely, passed to her ancestors and he married another woman. Now any possible vestige of Black Buffalo Woman disappears forever.

The family tree Edward Star shared with me shows another wife, Talks About Her, who may have succeeded Brings Plenty. The last, verifiable sighting of No Water himself is in July 1888, when he received annuity goods, including clothing. Thereafter, all is silence.

Of their descendants, there is a record of only Ivan Star Comes Out, born in 1875, grandfather of the present-day Edward Star. A scattering of No Waters appear sporadically in the Pine Ridge Reservation as well as the Rosebud Reservation censuses over the following years. It could be that they changed their name back to No Water or, more likely, they were different families altogether.

PERHAPS...

Just under a year after Crazy Horse's ill-fated 1869 spring buffalo hunt, the year that Crazy Horse's half-brother, Little Hawk, was killed, Black Buffalo Woman gave birth to a light-haired daughter who, according to all accounts, strongly resembled Crazy Horse. According to Ambrose, this daughter lived at the Pine Ridge Reservation till around World War II, though the provenance of this is unclear. He Dog, in his interview with Hinman, also confirmed she was alive in 1930, at the time of his interview, but declined to identify her.

This mysterious daughter is the greatest enigma of all, and her story could possibly be as fascinating as that of Anastasia, the lost daughter of Czar Nicholas II.

This is more than just idle speculation. Black Buffalo Woman always had a strong crush on Crazy Horse, as has been recounted by many contemporaries, and No Water's jealousy is equally well documented. That Crazy Horse reciprocated her feelings is confirmed by the various accounts of his warnings to No Water about his ill-treatment of her, as also his willingness to take her along on that fateful buffalo hunt.

That they shared a conjugal tipi during that hunt can be surmised with some confidence from He Dog's statement to Hinman that Crazy Horse "married" her, and even from his later, contradictory, claim that he had to return his Shirt because of "adultery." These observations, coupled with the passage of significantly less than a year to the birth, further make the point.

Finally, some oral family histories report that on her return to No Water by Red Cloud, she was made to live in a separate tipi nearby. Clearly, No Water, too, had little doubt about the nature of her relationship with the great warrior and wanted nothing to do with her physically. It is likely that this separation from the conjugal home endured for some time, as the fecund Black Buffalo Woman had another child only four years later, in 1874—if she is indeed, as I have reason to believe, the Black Crow living with No Water recorded in the Pine Ridge Census. While No Water's age tallies with his reported year of birth, Black Crow is five years younger than Black Buffalo Woman would have been. However, this is almost certainly the result of clerical error, as age in the censuses was pretty much a hit-or-miss affair. For example, in the very next census, in 1876, one child has aged a year, while the other has mysteriously aged two years in the same twelve-month period. Occasionally, an entire family of husband, wife and multiple children have exactly the same age! In some rolls, those listed have actually become much younger with the passing years. In the 1887 Census, for instance, Star Comes Out is fourteen years old but becomes seven years old in 1890 (the fact that he is listed with the same family members proves it is the same person).

While some of these blunders are obviously due to clerical sloppiness, others are more understandable, as it was not always easy to work out which year a Lakota was born in or even for them to be consistent about it, as it was not only reliant on memory, which does grow hazy with age, but also because the Lakota did not number the years. Instead, they remembered them for some memorable event, or events, that took place that year. These milestone events were usually drawn on cured deerskin called winter counts. The enumerators' difficulties were further compounded by the fact that, as explained by the Lakota author Joseph Marshall III, the annual calendar used by the Lakota was based on the thirteen lunar cycles, and so there were, logically, thirteen months. The names for months were based on events they experienced in Nature, eg. the Moon When the Ducks Come Back. Identities cannot, therefore, be determined based solely on their age.

Sadly, no traceable records exist today of this daughter or her descendants, who probably wish her to remain undisturbed, at peace, buried in obscurity. If true, this is a huge loss, as a DNA test on any descendent of this daughter could perhaps reveal a direct line to the great Chief Crazy Horse....

NELLIE

LARRABEE

TIMELINE FOR NELLIE LARRABEE

1853	Nellie Larrabee born
3 Aug 1877	Given to Crazy Horse
3 Sep 1877	Possible abduction
5 Sep 1877	Assassination of Crazy Horse
1878	Married Albert Greasy Hand
8 Jul 1928	Nellie Larrabee died

ELLEN "NELLIE" LARABEE

Much has been made of this brief episode in the life of Crazy Horse, though in truth it was of very little consequence. Her story is included here as she was one of the women associated with him, but, unlike the other two, she had no influence or impact on his life.

Nellie was born in 1853, near the South Platte River, the daughter of a minor French civilian trader based at Fort Robinson named "Long Joe" Larrabee and a Cheyenne wife whose name, in the best tradition of the times, was not considered worth recording for posterity. Nellie was the second of four daughters. By all accounts, Long Joe's ethics and moral integrity left something to be desired, and he spent more time doing odd jobs around the Fort, ingratiating himself with the soldiers, than any real trading. Few trusted him, though he did all he could to cultivate their favor.

By the beginning of August 1877, Red Cloud's insinuations and rumor-mongering had begun to cause significant suspicion and concern among the soldiers at Fort Robinson, as well as in their officers, about Crazy Horse's alleged intention to return to the warpath. While the man himself lived peaceably at his Lone Horn Camp and all who truly knew him understood that, as a Lakota warrior, he would never break his word, the Fort was agog in the belief that he and his followers were preparing to break out and restart the war. Only people without a syllabary understand the immutable value of a verbal commitment. It became increasingly clear to the Army that they needed ears inside the Lone Horn Camp, to gain real intelligence about the greatly feared Chief's plans. This intense fear is eloquent testimony to the Army's view of Crazy Horse.

At this point, ever on the lookout for ways to brown-nose the officers, Larrabee approached Lt. William Philo "White Hat" Clark with an offer to "gift" his attractive teenage daughter, Nellie, to Crazy Horse and use her as a spy, right inside his tipi. This otherwise intelligent and wise officer had by then been thoroughly poisoned against Crazy Horse by Red Cloud and readily acquiesced. On August 3, they brought her to his camp, while he was away at a council with Lt. Clark, convincing Black Shawl that she would help her with her household chores. On his return, Crazy Horse, with some reluctance, allowed her to stay when he heard she was willing to help care for his ailing wife. Black Shawl, confident in her husband's love for her, raised no objection to her presence. There is, however, no evidence whatsoever that he was ever married to her or even had any such intention, despite He Dog's, probably mistranslated, statement. His half-sister, Iron Cedar's recollections, too, do not mention any marriage. She dates Nellie's arrival around 2-4 August. Surprisingly, the usually accurate Bray claims Crazy Horse had an affair with her, then got Black Shawl's consent and married her, which is ridiculous and without any evidentiary basis whatsoever, besides not fitting either the timeframe or the man's character. More credibly, William Garnett, who witnessed all these events firsthand, observed that she was "a half-blood, not of the best frontier variety, an invidious and evil woman." Possibly a bit harsh on a young girl, but likely to be true considering her stock and upbringing.

To no one's surprise, Crazy Horse did not share any pillow talk with the young girl and she gleaned next to no intelligence of use to the Army. Only the ever-unreliable Bordeaux suggested that the veteran warrior took "advice" from this inexperienced teenager, an obviously ludicrous idea. Having failed in her mission, but still craving the soldiers' attention, like any giddy girl of her age, she made some things up and vastly exaggerated others in an effort to shore up her importance in this scheme. Without a doubt, her concoctions sowed more confusion and concern in an apprehensive and overwrought soldier population.

On September 3, the day before Crazy Horse took Black Shawl to the Spotted Tail Agency and two days before his assassination, the Fort Loafers abducted her back to their main camp, while Crazy Horse was out, according to Bray, quoting Eagle Elk. If this improbable event did indeed take place, the fact that Crazy Horse completely ignored it, to focus on the health and safety of Black Shawl clearly demonstrates her insignificance.

Within days of Crazy Horse's assassination, Nellie and her father ransacked his abandoned tipi and took everything they could lay their hands on, including his Ration Ticket. This action, too, reveals much about the nature of their relationship. The following year, 1878, Nellie married Albert Greasy Hand at Eagle Nest Butte in the Pine Ridge Reservation and settled among the Wajaje band, where she was known as Chi Chi or Brown Eyes Woman (Ista Gli Win).

Greasy Hand unscrupulously drew rations as Crazy Horse for at least six months, which speaks to how disorganized and chaotic Fort Robinson had become. In later years, he even tried calling himself Albert Crazy Horse but was quickly shut down by the entire Lakota community. Much later, in the summer of 1967 at a powwow, a descendent of this couple, calling himself Crazy Horse Bison, tried to claim direct descent from the famous war chief but was shown up as a fraud by the Edward Clown family members who happened to be present. The descendants of this couple still live around Eagle Nest Butte, in the Pine Ridge Reservation.

The Pine Ridge death records note that Ellen Nellie Larrabee died on July 8, 1928, at the ripe, old age of 75 years and was buried at the Wanblee Catholic Mission Cemetery, in Grave #2, within Section #15, not far from today's Crazy Horse School. Ironically, her life and death, which had such a brief and insignificant contact with Crazy Horse, are far better documented for posterity than those of the two women who did have a substantial impact on him, and over a considerably longer period.

RED
HERRING

TIMELINE FOR RED HERRING BLACK SHAWL

Prior to 1886 Red Horse widowed with 3 children, married Black Blanket

1887 Black Blanket now Blanket Black

2nd Son, Chasing Hawk, gone

1890 By now, stabilized as Black Shawl

3rd Son, Spotted Crow, gone

4th Daughter, Counting, becomes Weary

5th Son, Otter Skin becomes Otter

1891 4th Daughter, Weary, becomes Mary Red Horse

1892 Eldest Son, Ree, at Fort Meade

4th Daughter, Mary Red Horse, becomes Weary Again

1894 Eldest Son, Ree, becomes Ree Red Horse

5th Son, Otter becomes Russell Red Horse

1895 Eldest Son, Ree, gone

1897 Granddaughter, Horse, adds name Kate Red Horse

1901 4th Daughter, Weary married Kills Alive

Granddaughter, drops Horse name and gets married

1902 4th Daughter, Weary had son, James Kills Alive

1908 Red Horse died

1910 Russell Red Horse married Sophia Eagle Thunder

1911 Sophia Eagle Thunder died

1914 Russell Red Horse married Ellen Bear Growling/White Buffalo

1925 Black Shawl died

1933 Ellen Bear Growling died

RED HERRING

Many perils beset an amateur researcher—not the least of them being deciding where to begin! One of the major problems with history, and a poorly documented history at that, is the rather inconvenient fact that there is no clear beginning or end. As some wise person once remarked, history is a flowing river that waits for no man. And, as I discovered, some rivers rush, not flow!

Like manna in the desert, my hunt was saved from a sad, premature abortion by the discovery of the absolute treasure-trove that is the National Archives and Records Administration (NARA) facility of the United States, at Kansas City, Missouri. Not only does it hold whatever original records could be salvaged from that period, but they have also put in considerable effort to digitize some of them and even make them available freely on the Internet. This remarkable body, founded only in 1934, seriously underfunded and undermanned, has managed to save an amazing body of work that would have otherwise been completely lost to us. Sadly, quite a bit already has been, before NARA, and this is especially true of the records from the early days of the Agency period of the Dakotas.

Having discovered this motherlode on the Internet, I plunged in fearlessly, painstakingly navigating the bewildering labyrinth that is their catalogue system and, after months of searching, triumphantly uncovered a Census record for Black Shawl! Even her year of birth matched. It felt like reaching through a thick wall of fog and grasping a friendly hand. What I did not realize then, in my excitement, was that the digitization of these documents does not extend all the way to the critical 1876 to 1890 period, and I was therefore unwittingly beginning in the middle of the story. As a result, I would spend many months chasing a red herring—albeit a fascinating one! As it turned out, even red herrings can tell an alluring tale, glimpsed through the mists of time and decaying documents to offer a precious insight into their lives.

The earliest census records I could find, on microfilm, were for the year 1886, and scanning it online, it did not take me long to reach #309 and find "Black Blanket." In the 1887 Census, she becomes "Blanket Black," but by 1890 she is "Black Shawl." The age of this lady matches "our" Black Shawl's. However, my excitement at this quick discovery was tempered by the realization that the Census shows her as the wife of another man, Red Horse, with no fewer than six children! Of course, it was always possible that Black Shawl remarried after the assassination of Crazy Horse—a woman needed a male protector, if at all possible, in the days of the Wild West—and it did resonate with the expectation of her late husband's family, as mentioned in Victoria Conroy's letter. However, having studied her for years, I felt I had almost got to "know" her mind, and so this troubled me, aware as I was of her utter devotion to Crazy Horse and her youthful refusal to marry anyone else well into her 20s, most unusual in her society. Moreover, both Crazy Horse's dearest friend, He Dog, as well as her brother, Red Feather, are on record confirming that she never did remarry. A quandary.

My excitement at this "discovery" was so great that I brushed this niggling doubt aside and decided to map the travails of this not-so-little family. Studying the records proved that Black Shawl was clearly the second wife of Red Horse, his first having passed to her ancestors. This is evident from the ages of the three older children—sons, Ree, aged 30 years; Chasing Hawk, aged 29 years; and Spotted Crow, aged 25 years, in 1886, when she herself was only 41 years old. The next child, daughter Counting, is twelve years old that year, and the gap of thirteen years from Spotted Crow makes it unlikely that she was from the first wife, whereas a 28-year age gap to Black Shawl makes it probable she was hers. By the same logic, the last two children—son, Otter Skin, aged four years; and daughter, Horse, aged two years—could only be hers. So, she had married a widower with three children and then had three more of her own with him. This was really exciting, as it could mean that Black

Shawl's DNA may have come down to our own times, through the descendants of these last three children.

By 1887, Chasing Hawk is no longer in this family group, and it can be assumed that he had married and moved out to his new wife's tipi. Similarly, by 1890 Spotted Crow is also gone, presumably taking the same route of matrimony. Ree is recorded as having Ticket #309, living in Cherry Creek, close to the Touch the Clouds family. Curiously, though, he, the eldest son (becoming Ree Red Horse in 1894), continues in the family tipi till as late as 1895, when he too disappears. Prior to this, in 1892 a notation against his name states "At Fort Meade," which could mean he was a prisoner there for some reason or an enrolled scout, or even just away visiting someone thereabouts.

During this period, as often happened with Lakota names, the children's appellations underwent a gradual transformation, though father Red Horse and mother Black Shawl retained their names to the end. While their Census Roll #309 remains constant, in 1890 Counting became Weary—presumably, years of counting can make you so—though this Census makes her seventeen years old, while she had been eighteen in 1887. Throughout the myriad censuses, ages transform in astonishing ways for many people, and hence they are, at best, only an approximate guide to the real person. In 1891, she changed her name again, to Mary Red Horse, and returned to her earlier age of eighteen years. However, by 1892 she was Weary again and would remain so thereafter. She married Kills Alive, probably in 1901, and had a son, James Kills Alive, in 1902.

By 1890, Otter Skin had shed Skin and become just Otter. Then, from 1894 this changed to Russell Red Horse and remained that way thereafter. The last child, Horse, retained her name till 1897, when the Census records a second name for her, Kate Red Horse. For the first time, the 1892 Census enlightens us that she was actually a granddaughter, not a daughter, though being briefly nominated as the latter in the 1896 Census. She is likely to have been the daughter of either Chasing Hawk or Spotted Crow who, along with his wife, had probably died at some point, leaving her to the care of her grandparents, as was customary in Lakota society. It is unlikely to have been Ree (though theoretically his wife too may have died, leaving her) as he leaves the family tipi by 1895 while in his mid-30s without taking this child along.

Life seems to have continued placidly for the rest of the family, for some years. They each added a year, and little else seems to have happened till the turn of the century. In 1901, Kate Red Horse finally dropped the additional, solitary Horse moniker, and being eighteen years old then it is possible she got married that year and moved out to her own tipi, as she is missing from the family tipi in the next census, in 1902. The family circle now dwindles to just three. The previous year, Weary, too, had disappeared, married, leaving just Russell with his parents.

For some reason, the 1905 Census has a strange format and numbering, which makes it much more difficult to sift through.

The threesome live their lives, apparently peacefully, till 1907. But, in the next census, in 1909, there is a gaping hole. Red Horse is gone. He joined his ancestors on October 31, 1907, at the age of 71 years. Now just Black Shawl, a widow of 64 years, and Russell, her 27-year-old son, remain.

1910 was a year of celebration, as Russell finally brought a wife into the family. Sophia Eagle Thunder was 21 years old, and Black Shawl would have looked forward to seeing a grandchild from her. Tragically, however, she passed away soon after their marriage, and the following census shows Russell a widower at the age of just 27 years.

Black Shawl is missing in 1912 but appears again the following year. Perhaps she was away visiting relatives during the census. Russell married Ellen Bear Growling (also known as White Buffalo) in 1914. A grandchild, however, seems to have eluded her too, and in 1925 (as noted in the 1926 Census), at the age of eighty years, Black Shawl passed away. Eerily, she was born the same year as "our" Black Shawl, passed at the same age, in the same Cherry Creek/Bridger area, of the same Cheyenne River Reservation, living next to the same Waglula family members. So, was she really….

This is the watershed moment that led me to make a second pilgrimage to NARA in Kansas City. While a few nuggets of information needed rechecking and reconfirmation, the entire story of my favorite red herring needed corroboration, especially for those crucial years from which only a few tattered documents survive.

Russell and Ellen lived on together till 1933, when she died, possibly giving birth to a stillborn child, always a high risk in a geriatric pregnancy. Russell is again alone in the 1937 Census, a widower twice over.

It would be much later, after I had visited NARA, combed through original documents, and been able to trace a logical timeline for Black Shawl, that I realized this could not be "our" Black Shawl but another, contemporaneous person. The final, decisive nail in the coffin of this convenient storyline was the realization that the 1886 Census shows her married to Red Horse—at a time "our" Black Shawl, a widow, is clearly witnessed living with They Are Afraid of Her at Cheyenne River and then with her mother, Red Elk, at Pine Ridge. Such are the vagaries of hunting the ghosts of times gone by.

After some thought, I decided to include their census extracts here, along with their story, despite the risk of some confusion and uncertainty, to give voice to the misty tendrils of their tale, reaching out through crumbling vellum and onionskin, to share their lives, their joys, their sorrows, their triumphs and tragedies....

BACKSTORY

The dust devils chased each other crazily across the arid landscape, framed against a backdrop of stark, rocky mountains. The hot breath of Arabia whispered the death of the glorious Oman winter. Looking up, a startling strip of green grass, the Muscat Hills Golf Course, lay sandwiched between the two strips of brown sand and rock. Above it all, on the horizon, sparkled the azure Gulf of Oman, like icing on an especially alluring cake.

It was the summer of 2019, a year after my solo pilgrimage across the Native American heritage of the Great Plains. I had driven from Tulsa to the Yellowstone National Park, drifting through Oklahoma, Kansas, Nebraska, South Dakota, Wyoming and Montana, and visiting most of the major Native historical landmarks, however off-the-beaten-track, and every relevant museum and memorial during a month-long odyssey that would turn out to be one of the most memorable, moving and transformative experiences of my entire life. On my return I had found, somewhat to my astonishment, that my casual notes of the trip were copious and told a compelling story, all on their own! That eventually gave birth to my first "accidental" book, *Red Road Across the Great Plains*.

Sitting in my study at home in Muscat, in the Sultanate of Oman, I gazed across the unique landscape and ruminated. The two years of global isolation, caused by the Covid-19 pandemic, were yet to hit, as also was my tryst with colon cancer, both of which fortunately passed, in due course. They would, however, both result in serious delays to my research. Cancer trumped history, and the pandemic trampled travel. And, of course, writing at home begets its own perils, with unpredictable, constantly-erupting, minor domestic crises and alarms, like Vesuvius on steroids.

Savoring memories of my journey, a little at a time, every morsel full of riches, I eventually got to thinking of Crazy Horse and of the two women who played such a pivotal role in his life and even, indirectly, shaped the course of his career. His first love interest, Black Buffalo Woman, disappears from the pages of history shortly after the attempt on his life by her husband. His wife, Black Shawl, vanishes almost equally completely, a few years after his assassination at Fort Robinson. What became of them? How did their lives play out? Did they have descendants, perhaps living today? Did they ever find happiness again?

Understandably, they have been of limited or no interest to historians over the years, living as they did in the gigantic shadow of the legendary Crazy Horse, whose story is the very stuff of sagas. It is somehow fitting that an entire mountain is required to build a modern-day memorial to him in the sacred Black Hills he fought so hard to defend for his people, and it is unlikely that the sculptors take much notice of the fauna at its base, far, far below the peak. These women have effectively become footnotes to his story, if they appear at all. Knowing what I now do of them, I considered this historical oblivion grossly unfair and unjust, after the impactful roles they played in the great warrior's life. The more I thought about it, the more curious I became to uncover their stories.

The result of an enduring passion for Native American heritage, especially that of the northern Great Plains Nations, nurtured over half a century, my library has accumulated a large number of books, articles, videos and other items—including an authentic Pipe, handmade in Pipestone, Minnesota, at which I now gaze for inspiration. Everything remains enigmatic and silent, as though daring my resolve to battle the shadowy guardians of lost years.

The worst genocide in world history, and one of the least known, the 5,000,000 Native American population in 1500 C.E. was reduced to just 237,000 by 1900, as estimated by the official U.S. Census, devastated by a mind-boggling 95%. To put it in perspective (but in no way diminish its atrocity), Hitler's genocide of European Jewry wiped out about 60% of them, according to Yad Vashem. Today, after the passage of centuries, the Native American population has begun to recover a little, to almost 2,000,000, still only 40% of their number before they were "civilized" by the white man. Their destiny was remarkably similar to that of the buffalo they revered and depended upon. This American "conquest" was achieved, as David Truer points out, "more on the depth of its pockets than on the strength of its convictions." The bland indifference of modern Europeans to the deeds of their forebears was on full, shocking display when, for instance, in June 1992 replicas of Columbus' three ships sailed into New York Harbor, to celebrate "the friendship of the Spanish people." What rape and rapine, what torture, what slavery?

Amazingly, this trauma has not dented the undaunted Lakota sense of humor, though it is often laced with skeins of pain. Truer, again, relates an incident that demonstrates this well. Asked what should be done to the Kaiser, after the war was over (and reflecting on the [war] service of his own people and their subsequent treatment), an elderly Lakota man responded that the German leader should be "confined to a reservation, given an allotment, and forced to farm. When the Kaiser asked for help," the old man continued, "the Indian Agent should say to him, 'Now, you lazy, bad man, you farm and make your living by farming, rain or no rain, and if you do not make your own living, don't come to the Agency whining when you have no food in your stomach and no money, but stay here on your farm and grow fat till you starve.'" It speaks eloquently of a people who have been completely self-reliant for millennia and never wanted to be made dependent on the wasicu's handouts anyway. Indeed, many of the Nations had been farmers long before the Europeans; the Wampanoag Nation had even enabled the hapless Pilgrims off the *Mayflower* to survive by showing them how to grow corn and other crops! A favor the settlers promptly repaid by enslaving or killing them. Such instances are liberally scattered throughout their saga—the "generous" gift of blankets to one tribe, liberally infected with smallpox; the invitation to another for a "thanksgiving" feast, to be summarily butchered; even Andrew Jackson, whose life was saved by a Cherokee warrior, Junaluska, at the Battle of Horseshoe Bend, repaying them with his inhuman Trail of Tears. A pitiless destiny, indeed. And, through the unending pain, their courage and resilience has endured, to smile. Remarkable.

In another instance of Native humor laced with the pain of reality, in 1973 an Ojibwe, Adam Nordwall, flew to Italy in full regalia and claimed the country "by right of discovery." Apparently, Europeans were not amused.

During my solo road trip, I had stayed in a tepee on the Pine Ridge Reservation and I recall my hostess showing me an electrified fence to keep wild horses out, asking me, deadpan, "Want to touch it?"

This irrepressible sense of fun comes through even in some of the names given to census officers. There are many instances of the Lakota clearly amusing themselves at the expense of their oblivious captors. Obviously fake names abound, such as Harlot (listed as a wife), Whore, Son of a Skunk, Crotch, Smells Bad, Married Temporarily, Bad Woman, Red Crack (another wife), Kiss Me, Chamber Pot, Pain on Rump, Rotten Woman, Ugly Old Woman, Puke (his eleven-year-old daughter was Rosa Puke), Prick Face, Skins His Penis, Testicle Head, No Name, Waste, and many more that are scurrilous enough to make a publisher blush.

As Crazy Horse had predicted about the seventh generation, today, the Lakota are slowly winning again, though not through arms and battle as of yore. Efforts such as that of Lakota Chef Sean Sherman (the Sioux Chef), who makes authentic indigenous foods with local, pre-colonial ingredients and whose new restaurant, Owamni, in Minneapolis, has been voted the best new restaurant in America, are slowly beginning to take over the hearts—and stomachs—if not yet all the minds, of the descendants of the white invaders. Today, there are notable Native fashion models, famous Hollywood actors, U.S. Cabinet ministers, astronauts, and much more. A member of the Kaw Nation has even served as the 31st Vice President of the United States. The day may yet dawn when we see a Native American as President. The Red Road would come around full circle.

The census rolls themselves provide a fascinating insight into the minds of the enumerators and their superiors. The point at which the typewriter was invented is evident, replacing ink and even pencil records. Racism, of course, comes through clear and strong, in various forms, among them being references to "Whites and Other People," as also the fact that "Mrs." was added only to the names of married European females but not to that of any Native wife. In fact, marriage registers regularly recorded the names of white wives but only "Indian" or "half-breed" or even "h.b." for others, destined to remain faceless forever. While some were very painstaking, writing in exquisite copperplate that can be admired even today, others were careless and haphazard, clearly indifferent to their task. Yet others added little gossipy notes here and there, which provide flashes of their domestic life.

The challenge for any researcher into Native American history is considerably intensified by their naming convention, which makes it incredibly difficult to trace many lineages. Not only did the Lakota change their name, often several times, during their lifetime, in response to particular events, choices, or visions, they were often conferred the name of their parent or grandparent, usually having earned the distinction with deeds of exceptional bravery. Thus, for example, the famed Crazy Horse was the third of his family to bear that name, having already had several other names earlier. Moreover, as their names were often based on the Nature they experienced or plants or animals seen during one of their intense vision quests, it led to some names being very common, though not quite as pedestrian as "John Smith."

The difficulties are further exacerbated by the fact that many records were lost over the centuries (or in some cases, I believe, intentionally destroyed by the U.S. Army or Indian Agents, in the long-ago), before NARA came into existence. Even some of the records that have survived, on crumbling vellum or onionskin, have parts of crucial pages damaged or no longer legible. Gaps in documentation for the crucial years have to be filled by referencing other sources, such as the movement of close family groups, oral histories, or even throwaway comments of major historians and narrators who did not attach much significance to these minor sidelines to their principal person of interest, but which sometimes turned out to be vital, pointed indicators for my purpose, like brief flashes of light glimpsed in a dark tunnel.

As with every coin, there is always a flip side and I cannot but enthusiastically admire the United States for not only rescuing whatever it could but also for having no hesitation in "telling it like it is, warts and all." At many of the historical sites, I was amazed to find the Rangers' narrative made no attempt to gloss over the genocide and had no thought for sparing white sensitivities. With an epic such as this, that takes immense courage and integrity, and I know of very few countries that can match this shining example. Even more amazing is how freely access to these precious old documents has been made available to all, including foreigners and those with no claim to academic or research credentials. Some of the material has even been digitized and made accessible on the Internet, despite this sometimes-overlooked Department's considerably constrained resources. This effort cannot be acclaimed enough and is a substantial contribution to the preservation of our common human heritage.

As for the travails of the Native Nations, it is past time that the dust of obscurity and shameless Hollywood misinformation was removed and the true tale told extensively, to America as well as the world—not to shame, or blame, the innocent descendants of blameworthy ancestors, but to come to terms with their inhumanity, make amends where practicable, and move forward, hopefully toward a brighter, shared tomorrow. Condemning these true "Lords of the Plains" to communities that are the poorest, unhealthiest and, above all, most bereft of hope in the entire country is a deeply shameful blot on the achievements of the wealthiest and most powerful nation on earth—justly deserving admiration for something never before achieved in just two centuries, in the entire history of humankind. It is, however, well past time to make up for the sins of the past.

Pila maya.

MAPS, PHOTOGRAPHS, DOCUMENTS, FAMILY TREES

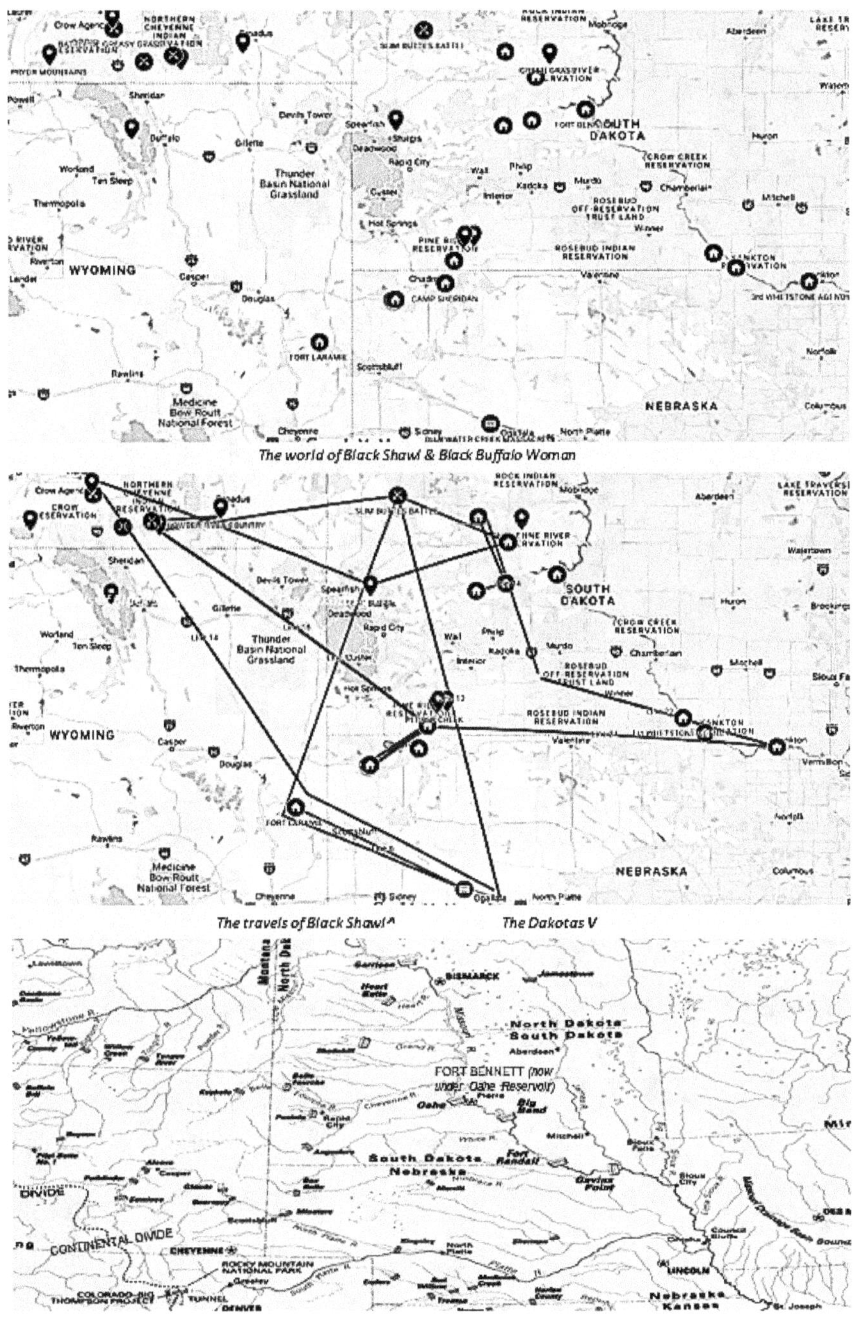

The world of Black Shawl & Black Buffalo Woman

The travels of Black Shawl ∧   The Dakotas ∨

MONTANA
NORTH
KOTA
MINNESO
Minn
H
G
F
WYOMI
B
E
C
NEB SK
ake City
Denver
United States
IO
TRIBES
OF THE
INDIAN NATION
Blackfoot
Cree
Crow
Sioux
Paiute
Shoshone
Cheyenne
Ute
Pawnee
Navajo
Shawnee
Cherokee
Apache
Choctaw
Apache
Seminole

Author and his wife at the National Archives, Kansas City, Missouri

Black Shawl

Black Buffalo Woman

Marker at the site of the assassination of Chief Crazy Horse, at Fort Robinson — a poignant memorial of a dastardly deed by lesser men.

No Water

Ration Tickets

Nellie Larrabee

Ellen "Nellie" *Larabee* Crazy Horse

BIRTH	1853
DEATH	8 Jul 1928 (aged 74–75)
	Pine Ridge, Oglala Lakota County, South Dakota, USA
BURIAL	Catholic Mission Cemetery
	Wanblee, Jackson County, South Dakota, USA
PLOT	Grave # 2 – Section # 15
MEMORIAL ID	13090554 · View Source

Details of Ellen "Nellie" Larabee's grave ∧

∨ Spotted Tail's daughter, Hinzinwin's funerary scaffold at Fort Laramie

Crazy Horse—dead—killed by a bayonet stab while attempting to escape from custody at Red Cloud on the night of the 5th and 6th ult. He was an extraordinary savage, a spiritual medium and religious enthusiast. "He had only one wife, and his morals had so stiff an edge," says a writer in the *Tribune*, "that he never permitted himself to gain any personal advantage from his power. His cheek bones were not high; his features were small and delicate; his expression was gentle and sad: he was taciturn and absent minded. He was six feet in height, slender, light in color, and about thirty-two years old. Reckless daring on the war path, and a magnetic influence over his fellows, gave him prominence over the hostile Sioux."

Above: The assassination of Chief Crazy Horse, Fort Robinson

Right: Possible image of Waglula/Worm, Crazy Horse's father

Left: The United States honors its greatest adversary

Chief Touch the Clouds in 1877

Black Shawl in Census Index

Letter from War Department acknowledging Custer's early death in the battle

WAR DEPARTMENT
RESERVE OFFICERS' TRAINING CORPS
THE STATE UNIVERSITY OF IOWA
IOWA CITY

November 2, 1935

My dear Colonel Welch:

Your intensely interesting letter arrived yesterday and I have been analyzing the information given by you.

1. After thinking it over, I believe that it is more than likely that Custer was killed as you say, in the first part of the fight when he tried to cross the ford. Custer always rode at the head of his column and as the two leading men, officers you say, were killed, it is more than a mere probability that they were Custer and Captain Cook perhaps. The question now arises as to how would General Custer's body come to be on the knoll at the top of the hill?

2. As you have observed by actual visit to the field, there is no vegetation to speak of on the entire field. Do you have any information regarding the statement that at the time of Custer's fight there was a high growth of sagebrush reaching to the men's shoulders, which was later destroyed by sheep which were driven on to the range some years later?

3. Your letter stated that you thought the fight lasted 27 minutes "from the firing of the first shot by Reno's men until the last man was killed in Custer's outfit ". All the information seems to lead to the fact that Reno was engaged at the least, 45 minutes, from the time he formed his first line until he crossed the river on his retreat. It would seem to me that Custer would not have made a great deal more progress in a Northerly direction than Reno, and as Custer had some little distance farther to go in order to reach the ford, and further, that Reno was on the present Reno's Hill when he heard the volleys which were evidently fired by Custer's detachment--it does not all seem to fit in with the 27 minutes from the firing of the first shot by Reno. Can you enlighten me on the matter?

4. Now you said that Chief Gaul and Grass were not in on the Custer killing. Will you amplify this as much as you can without your notes?

5. What do you know about Sitting Bull's taking to the hills at the beginning of the fight?

6. Your analysis of the amount of amunition in the hands of the Indian appeals to me as I had never considered the fact of their having shot a large part of it in their fight with Crook the week before, and of course they had no opportunity to replenish it.

7. What is your estimate of the number of fighting braves in the entire village?

8. Have you read that squaw's account of the battle which has been edited by Marquis of Sheridan, Wyoming, and is on sale at the battlefield? If so, do you believe her statement that Custer had married or lived with this young woman squaw, as stated in the first part of the story?

9. When did Custer have time to cut his hair on the morning of the 25th and do you know why he did so?

I should like very much to look over your records if you could get them to me, and I assure you I shall return them as soon as I have examined them. I expect to make a talk in Cedar Rapids, Iowa, some time in December on this subject.

Thanking you again for your prompt reply, I am

Yours sincerely,

George F. M. Dailey,
Lt-Colonel, Infantry,
P. M. S. & T.

GFMD:drk

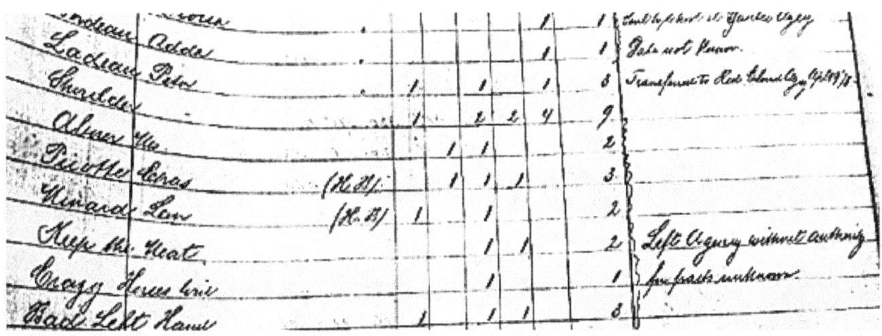

"Crazy Horse Wife" left Rosebud in 1877 "for parts unknown"

Black Shawl's Death Record, and Death Certificate, Cheyenne River Reservation 1925

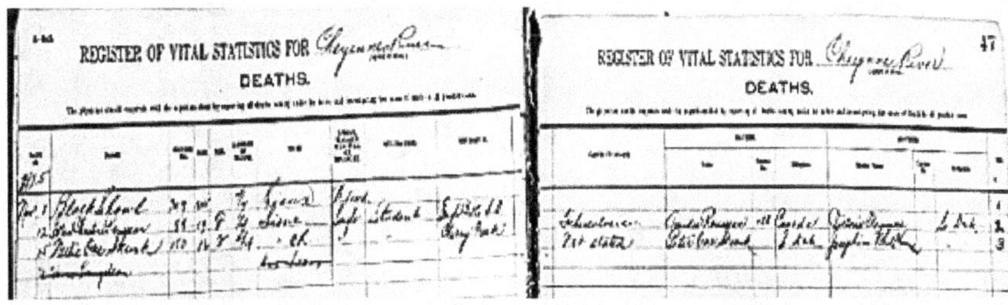

Register of Births & Deaths, listing Black Shawl 1825

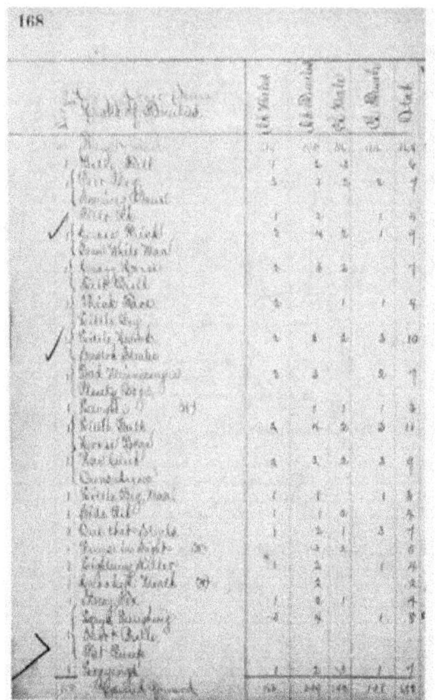

Crazy Horse Surrender Ledger

Curious names in the Censuses

Very old records still legible   Others had sloppy penmanship

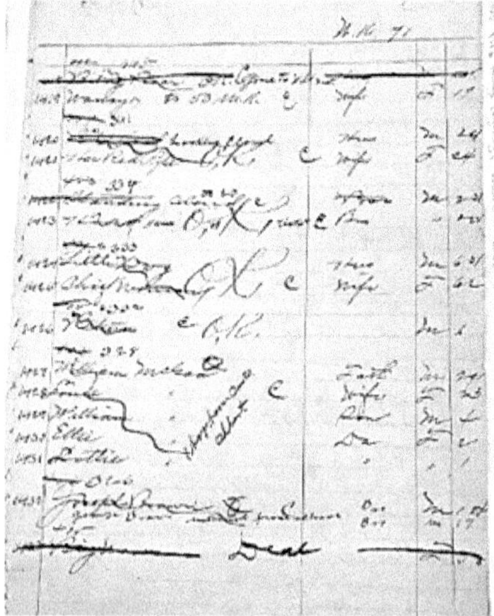

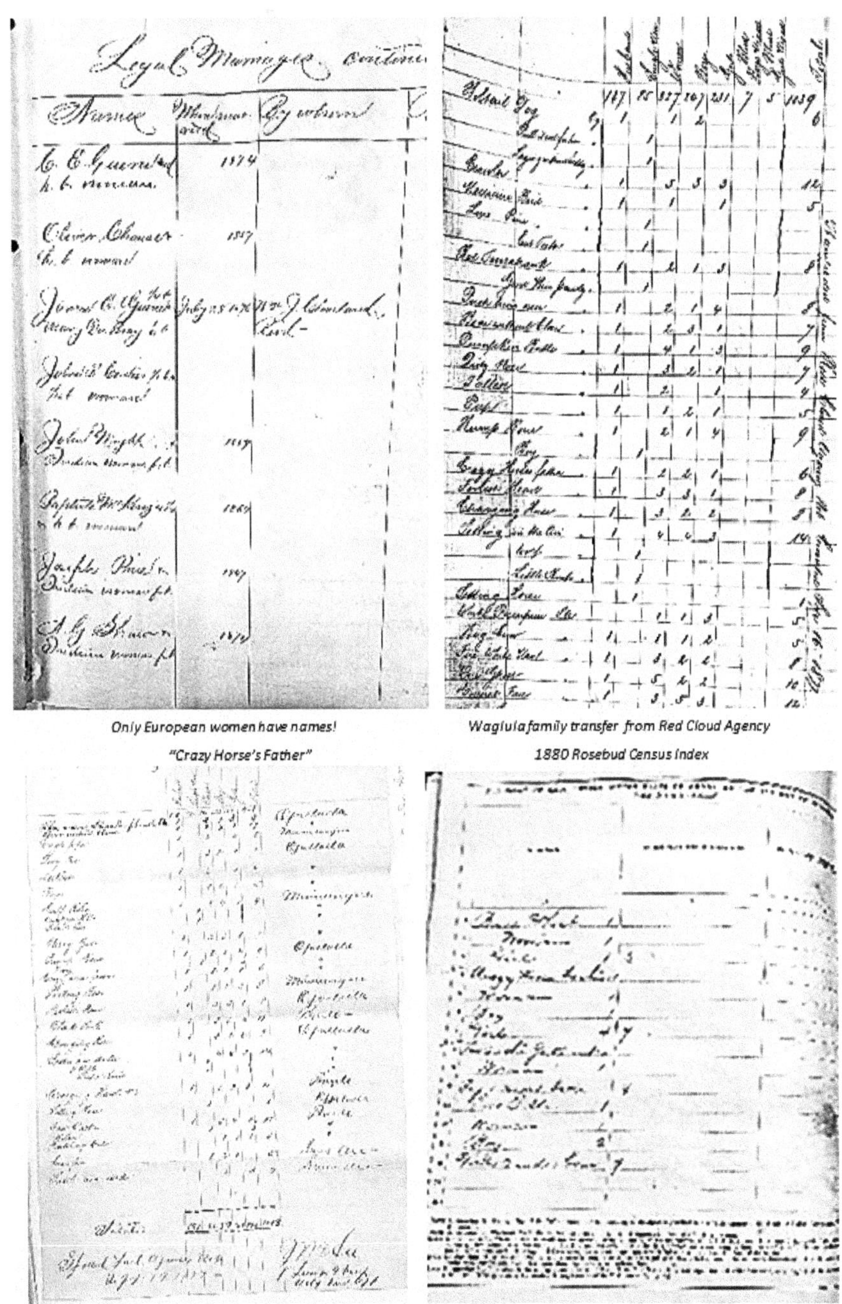

Only European women have names!

Waglula family transfer from Red Cloud Agency

"Crazy Horse's Father"

1880 Rosebud Census Index

Above & left : Condition of some old records inherited by NARA

Below : Some interesting names from the Census Rolls

Tells Lies — 3
Rotten Woman — 3
Mean Woman — 3

2740	Harlot		Wife	F	36
607	Son of a Skunk		Father	M	21
2854	Crotch		Wife	F	23
1883	Smell bad		Wife	F	64
2314	Married Temporarily		"	M	10
2377	Friendless			F	76
2702	Kill with Child on her back		Daughter	F	6

Red Crack — F — Wife — 28
Chamber Pot — M — Son — 8
Bad Looking Woman — F — 81
Pain in Rump — M — Fath. — 34

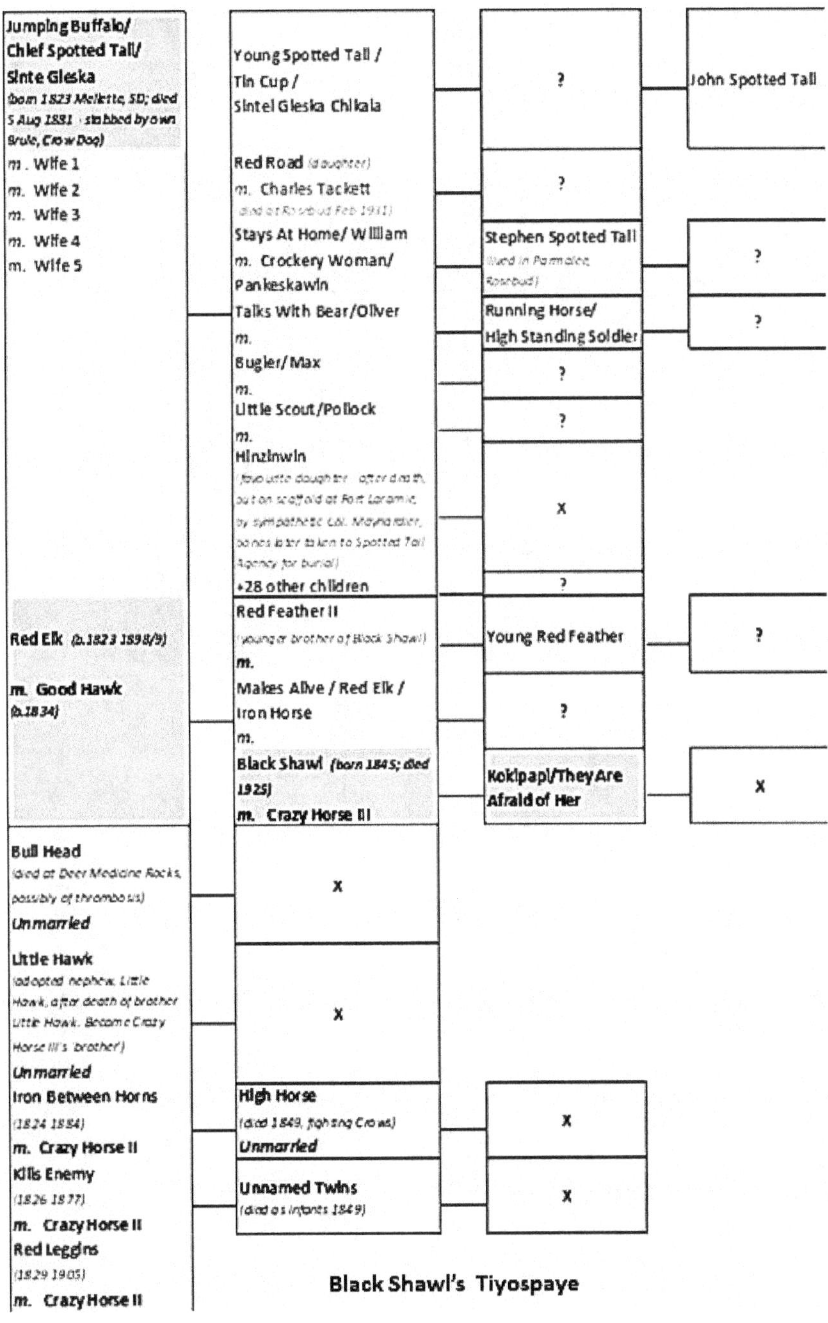
Jumping Buffalo/
Chief Spotted Tail/
Sinte Gleska
(born 1823 Mellette, SD; died
5 Aug 1881 - stabbed by own
Brule, Crow Dog)
m. Wife 1
m. Wife 2
m. Wife 3
m. Wife 4
m. Wife 5

Young Spotted Tail /
Tin Cup /
Sintei Gleska Chikala

Red Road (daughter)
m. Charles Tackett
(died at Rosebud Feb 1941)
Stays At Home/ William
m. Crockery Woman/
Pankeskawin
Talks With Bear/Oliver
m.
Bugler/Max
m.
Little Scout/Pollock
m.
Hinzinwin
(favourite daughter - after death,
put on scaffold at Fort Laramie,
by sympathetic Col. Maynadier,
bones later taken to Spotted Tail
Agency for burial)
+28 other children

Red Feather II
(younger brother of Black Shawl)
m.
Makes Alive / Red Elk /
Iron Horse
m.
Black Shawl (born 1845; died
1925)
m. Crazy Horse III

?
John Spotted Tall

?

Stephen Spotted Tall
(lived in Parmelee,
Rosebud)
Running Horse/
High Standing Soldier
?

?

X

?

Young Red Feather
?

X

?

?

?

Kokipapi/They Are
Afraid of Her

X

Red Elk (b.1823 1898/9)

m. Good Hawk
(b.1834)

Bull Head
(died at Deer Medicine Rocks,
possibly of thrombosis)
Unmarried

Little Hawk
(adopted nephew, Little
Hawk, after death of brother
Little Hawk. Became Crazy
Horse III's 'brother')
Unmarried
Iron Between Horns
(1824 1884)
m. Crazy Horse II
Kills Enemy
(1826 1877)
m. Crazy Horse II
Red Leggins
(1829 1905)
m. Crazy Horse II

X

X

High Horse
(died 1849, fighting Crows)
Unmarried
Unnamed Twins
(died as infants 1849)

X

X

Black Shawl's Tiyospaye

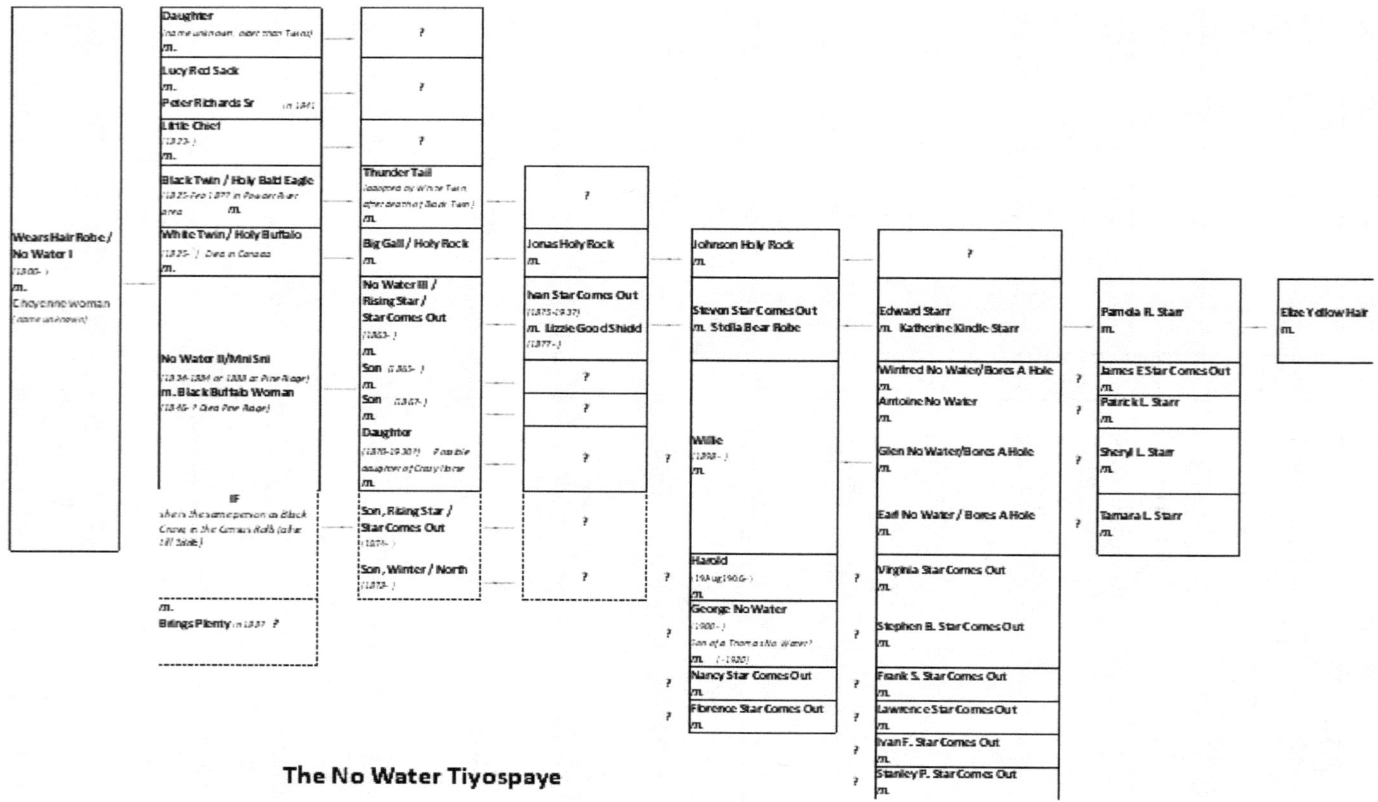
Wears Hair Robe / No Water I
(1800-)
m.
Cheyenne woman
(name unknown)

Daughter
(name unknown, older than Twins)
m.

Lucy Red Sack
m.
Peter Richards Sr   in 1841

Little Chief
(1823-)
m.

Black Twin / Holy Bald Eagle
(1825-Feb 1877 in Powder River area)
m.

White Twin / Holy Buffalo
(1825-) Died in Canada
m.

No Water II/Mini Sni
(1834-1884 or 1888 at Pine Ridge)
m. Black Buffalo Woman
(1846-? Died Pine Ridge)

IF
where is the same person as Black Crow in the Census Rolls (alive till 1908)
m.
Brings Plenty in 1837 ?

?

?

?

Thunder Tail
(adopted by White Twin after death of Black Twin)
m.

Big Gall / Holy Rock
m.

No Water III /
Rising Star /
Star Comes Out
(1863-)
m.
Son (1865-)
m.
Son (1867-)
m.
Daughter
(1870-1930?)   Possible daughter of Crazy Horse
m.

Son, Rising Star /
Star Comes Out
(1874-)

Son, Winter / North
(1872-)

?

Jonas Holy Rock
m.

Ivan Star Comes Out
(1875-1937)
m. Lizzie Good Shield
(1877-)

?

?

?

?

?

Johnson Holy Rock
m.

Steven Star Comes Out
m. Stella Bear Robe

Willie
(1908-)
m.

Harold
(19 Aug 1906-)
m.

George No Water
(1900-)
Son of a Thomas No Water?
m. (?-1920)

Nancy Star Comes Out
m.

Florence Star Comes Out
m.

?

Edward Starr
m. Katherine Kindle Starr

Winfred No Water/Bores A Hole
m.

Antoine No Water
m.

Glen No Water/Bores A Hole
m.

Earl No Water / Bores A Hole
m.

Virginia Star Comes Out
m.

Stephen B. Star Comes Out
m.

Frank S. Star Comes Out
m.

Lawrence Star Comes Out
m.

Ivan F. Star Comes Out
m.

Stanley P. Star Comes Out
m.

Pamela R. Starr
m.

James E Star Comes Out
m.

Patrick L. Starr
m.

Sheryl L. Starr
m.

Tamara L. Starr
m.

Elize Yellow Hair
m.

The No Water Tiyospaye

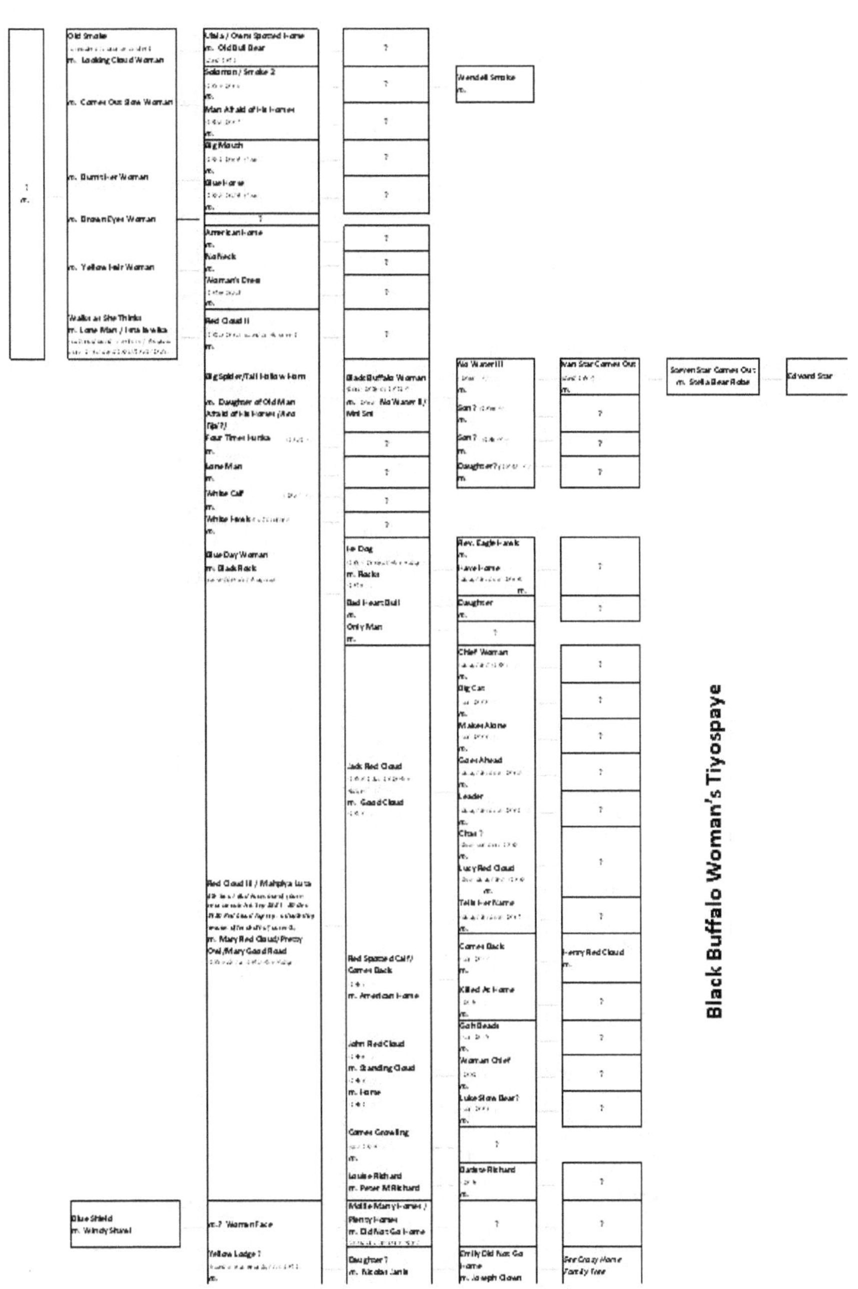
Black Buffalo Woman's Tiyospaye

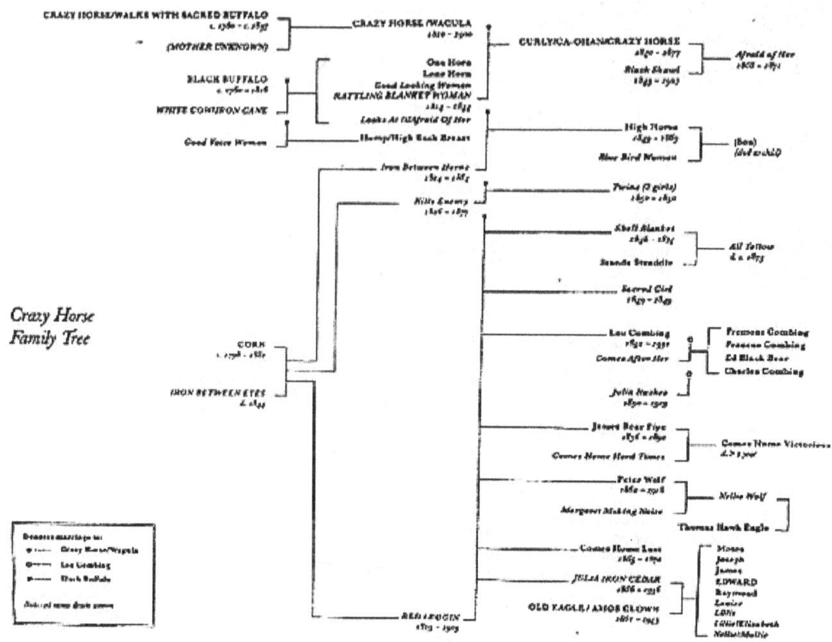

Above: The Crazy Horse Tiyospaye (courtesy Edward Clown Family & W. Matson)
Below: 'Red Herring' Black Shawl Tiyospaye

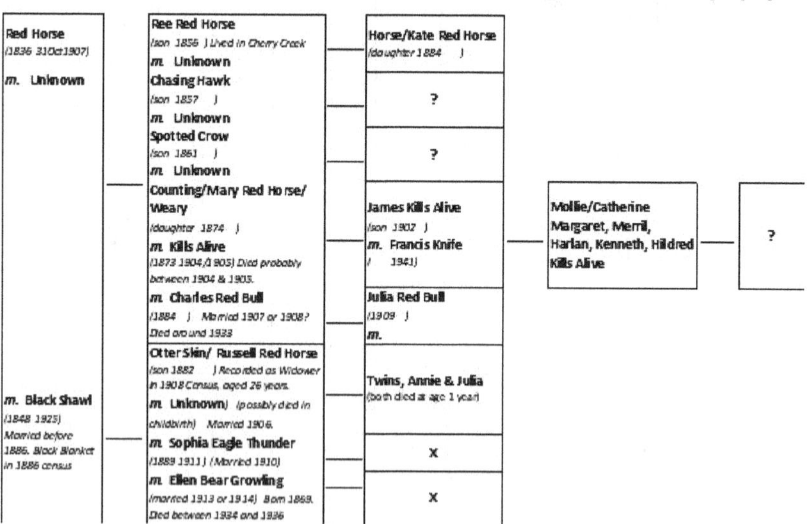

CENSUS

RECORDS

Waglula (Breast of Female) and family at Cheyenne River

No. 359 Breast of Female
Breast of Female   M 61 yrs old
Red Legs   F 61 " "
Iron Cedar   F 18 " "

Cheyenne River Reservation 1886

No. 351 Breast of Female
Breast of Female   M 63 yrs old
Red Leg   F 62 "
Iron Cedar   F 17 "

Cheyenne River Reservation 1887

No. 359 Breast of Female
Breast of Female   M 65
Red Legs   F 65

Cheyenne River Reservation 1890

no. 359
Breast of Female
1334 Breast of Female   M Head 66
1335 Red Legs   F wife 66

Cheyenne River Reservation 1891

1169 Breast of Female   M Husband 67
1170 Red Leg   F Wife 67

Cheyenne River Reservation 1892

1123 Breast of Female   M Husband 69
1124 Red Leg   F wife 69

Cheyenne River Reservation 1894

1226 Breast of Female   M 70
1227 Red Leg   F wife 70

Cheyenne River Reservation 1895

NUMBER.	INDIAN NAME.	ENGLISH NAME.	SEX.	RELATION.	AGE.
1223	Breass of Female		M.	Husband	72
1224	Red Log		F	wife	72

Cheyenne River Reservation 1896

NUMBER.	INDIAN NAME.	ENGLISH NAME.	SEX.	RELATION.	AGE.
1200		Breast of Female	M		72
1201		Red Log	F	Wife	72

Cheyenne River Reservation 1897

NUMBER.	INDIAN NAME.	ENGLISH NAME.	SEX.	RELATION.	AGE.
1208		Breast of Female	M.	Husband	73
1209		Red Log	F.	wife	73

Cheyenne River Reservation 1898

NUMBER.	INDIAN NAME.	ENGLISH NAME.	SEX.	RELATION.	AGE.
1199	Breast of Female		M.	Husband	74
1200	Red Log		F.	wife	74

Cheyenne River Reservation 1899

NUMBER.	INDIAN NAME.	ENGLISH NAME.	SEX.	RELATION.	AGE.
1190	Breast of Female		M.	Husband	75
1191	Red Log		F.	Wife	75

Cheyenne River Reservation 1900

NUMBER.	INDIAN NAME.	ENGLISH NAME.	SEX.	RELATION.	AGE.
1157		Breast of Female	M	Husb	76
1158		Red Log	F	Wife	76

Cheyenne River Reservation 1901

NUMBER.	INDIAN NAME.	ENGLISH NAME.	SEX.	RELATION.	AGE.
1151	Red Log		F.	woman	77

Cheyenne River Reservation 1902

NUMBER.	INDIAN NAME.	ENGLISH NAME.	SEX.	RELATION.	AGE.
1154	Red Log (Mrs Breast of Female)		F.	widow	78

Cheyenne River Reservation 1903

NUMBER.	INDIAN NAME.	ENGLISH NAME.	SEX.	RELATION.	AGE.
1140		Red Log (Mrs Breast of Female)	F	widow	79

Cheyenne River Reservation 1904

Black Shawl and Red Elk at Pine Ridge

977 Red Elk — Mother — ♀ 67
978 Her black blanket — Daughter — ♀ 43

Pine Ridge Reservation 1887

379
1566 Red Elk — Mother — ♀ 68
1567 Her Blanket — Daughter — 47

Pine Ridge Reservation 1888

274
Hehaka luta — Red Elk — ♀ mot 70.
Tasina sapa win — Her Black Blanket — ♀ da 46

Pine Ridge Reservation July 1, 1890

1332
1252 Onpan luta — Red Elk — f mot 70
1253 Sina sapa — Black Shawl — f da 40
1254 Niya pi — Make Alive — m son 18

Pine Ridge Reservation July 1, 1892

323
1256 — Red Elk — f mot 70
1257 — Black Shawl — f da 40
1258 — Make Alive — m son 18

Pine Ridge Reservation July 1, 1893

359
398 Hehaka luta — Red Elk — f Moth 72
399 Sina sapa — Black Shawl — f Da 42

Pine Ridge Reservation July 1, 1894

559
2171 Hehaka Luta — Red Elk — f Mother 73
2172 Sina Sapa — Black Shawl — f Da. 43

Pine Ridge Reservation June 30, 1895

35
1117 Sina Sapa — Black Shawl — F Head 47

Pine Ridge Reservation 1899

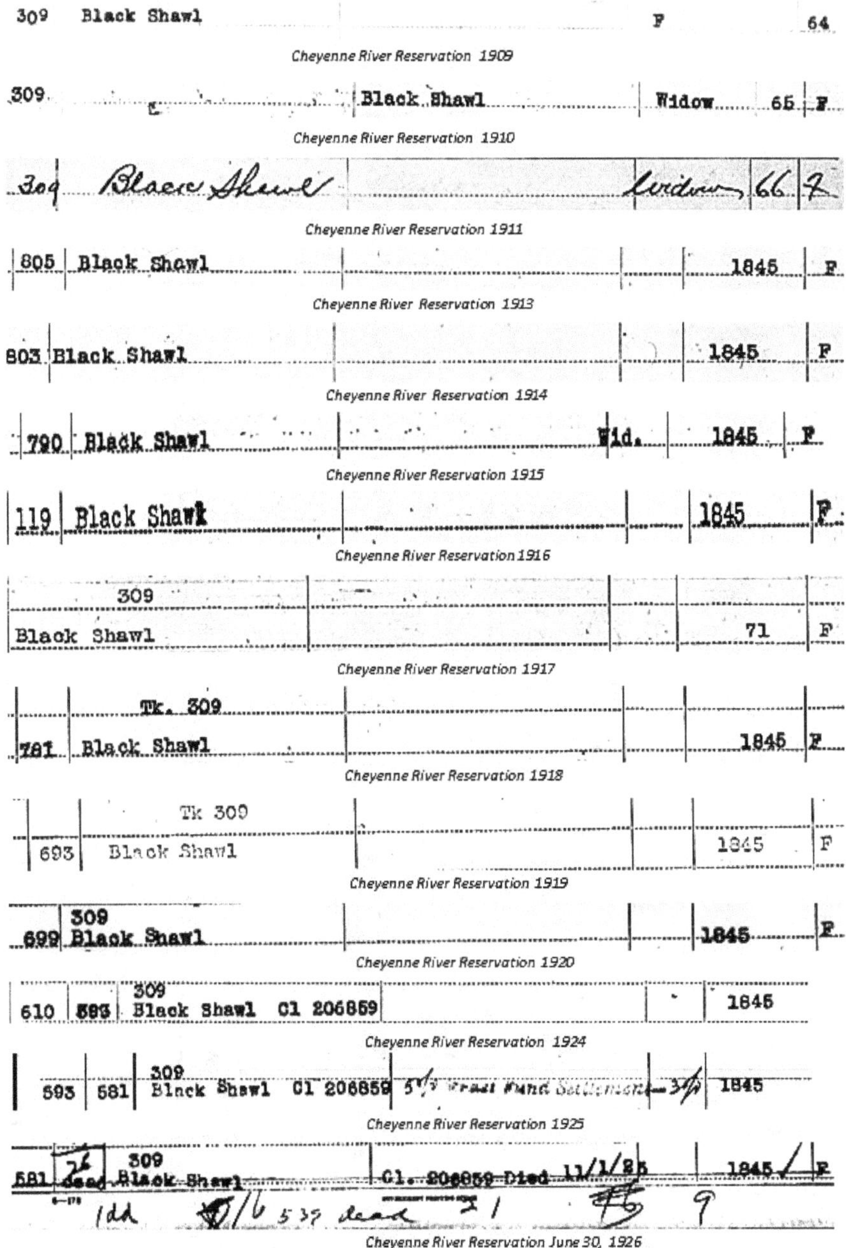

309   Black Shawl   F   64

Cheyenne River Reservation 1909

309 .... Black Shawl .... Widow ..... 65 . F

Cheyenne River Reservation 1910

309   Black Shawl   widow   66 F

Cheyenne River Reservation 1911

805 | Black Shawl   1845 | F

Cheyenne River Reservation 1913

803 | Black Shawl   1845   F

Cheyenne River Reservation 1914

790 | Black Shawl   Wid. | 1845 | F

Cheyenne River Reservation 1915

119 | Black Shawl   1845   F

Cheyenne River Reservation 1916

309
Black Shawl   71   F

Cheyenne River Reservation 1917

Tk. 309
781 | Black Shawl   1845 F

Cheyenne River Reservation 1918

Tk 309
693 | Black Shawl   1845   F

Cheyenne River Reservation 1919

309
699 | Black Shawl   1845   F

Cheyenne River Reservation 1920

610 | 583 | 309
Black Shawl   Cl 206859   1845

Cheyenne River Reservation 1924

593 | 581 | 309
Black Shawl   Cl 206859   5% Trust Fund Settlement—3%   1845

Cheyenne River Reservation 1925

581 | dead | 309
Black Shawl   Cl. 206859 Died 11/1/85   1845 / F

Cheyenne River Reservation June 30, 1926

No Water family at Pine Ridge

Pine Ridge Reservation 1886

Pine Ridge Reservation 1887

Pine Ridge Reservation 1888

Pine Ridge Reservation 1890

Pine Ridge Reservation 1892

Pine Ridge Reservation 1895

Pine Ridge Reservation 1899

Pine Ridge Reservation 1922

'RED HERRING' BLACK SHAWL AT CHEYENNE RIVER

Cheyenne River Census 1887

Cheyenne River Census 1890

Cheyenne River Census 1891

Cheyenne River Census 1892

1014	Red Horse	M	Husband	61
1015	Black Shawl	F	Wife	49
1016	Rus Red Horse	M	Son	35
1017	Weary	F	Daughter	20
1018	Russel Red Horse	M	Son	12
1019	Horse	F	Gd Daughter	10

Cheyenne River Census 1894

1053	Red Horse		M		62
1054	Black Shawl		F	wife	50
1055	Weary		F	daughter	21
1056	Russel Red Horse		M	son	13
1057	Horse		F	Gd. daughter	11

Cheyenne River Census 1895

1047	Red Horse		M	Husband	64
1048	Black Shawl		F	wife	52
1049	Weary		F	Daughter	23
1050	Russel Red Horse		M	Son	15
1051	Horse		F	Daughter	13

Cheyenne River Census 1896

1032	Red Horse	M		64
1033	Black Shawl	F	Wife	52
1034	Weary	"	Dau.	23
1035	Russel Red Horse	M	son	15
1036	Horse (Kate Red Horse)	F	G. Dau	13

Cheyenne River Census 1897

10 36	Red Horse	M	Husband	65
10 37	Black Shawl	F	wife	53
10 38	Weary	"	daughter	24
10 39	Russel Red Horse	M	Son	16
10 40	Horse (Kate Red Horse)	F	Gd daughter	14

Cheyenne River Census 1898

No.	Name	Sex	Relationship	Age
1025	Red Horse	M	Husband	66
1026	Black Shawl	F	wife	52
1027	Weary	F	daughter	25
1028	Russell Red Horse	M	son	
1029	Horse (Kate Red Horse)	F	grand-daughter	16

Cheyenne River Census 1899

No.	Name	Sex	Relationship	Age
1017	Red Horse	m.	Husband	67
1018	Black Shawl	F.	Wife	55
1019	Weary	F.	Dau.	26
1020	Russell Red Horse	m	Son	18
1021	Horse (Kate Red Horse	F.	Gd. Dau.	16

Cheyenne River Census 1900

No.	Name	Sex	Relationship	Age
990	Red Horse	M	Hust.	68
991	Black Shawl	F	Wife	56
992	Weary	F	Dau.	27
993	Russell Red Horse	M	Son	20
994	Kate Red Horse	F	Gd Dau.	17

Cheyenne River Census 1901

No.	Name	Sex	Relationship	Age
991	Red Horse	m	Hust.	69
992	Black Shawl	F	wife	57
993	Weary	F	Dau	78
994	Russell Red Horse	m	Son	20

Cheyenne River Census 1902

No.	Name	Sex	Relationship	Age
975	Red Horse	m.	Hust.	70
976	Black Shawl	F.	wife	58
977	Russell Red Horse	m.	Son	21

Cheyenne River Census 1903

No.	Name	Sex	Relationship	Age
969	Red Horse	m	Hust.	71
970	Black Shawl	F	wife	59
971	Russell Red Horse	m	Son	22

Cheyenne River Census 1904

No.		Name	Sex	Relationship	Age
922	309	Red Horse		Hust.	72
923	309	Black Shawl	Female	wife	60
924	309	Russell Red Horse	Male	Son	22

Cheyenne River Census 1905

209		Red Horse		m	Husb	72
		Black Shawl		f	Wife	61
		Russell Red Horse		m	Son	24

Cheyenne River Census 1906

309	Red Horse		m		74
	Black Shawl		F	Wife	62
843	Russell Red Horse		M		25
			F		Sioux

Cheyenne River Census 1907

| 309 | Black Shawl | | F | | 64 |
| 843 | Russell Red Horse | | M | | 27 |

Cheyenne River Census 1909

309		Black Shawl	Widow	65	F
843		Russell Red Horse		28	M
		Sophia Eagle Thunder	Wife	21	F

Cheyenne River Census 1910

| 309 | Black Shawl | | Widow | 66 | F |
| 843 | Red Horse | Russell | Widow | 29 | M |

Cheyenne River Census 1911

| 843 | 843 | Red Horse, Russell | widower | 30 |

Cheyenne River Census 1912   (Black Shawl missing)

| 803 | Black Shawl | | 1845 | F |
| 2294 | Russell Red Horse | | 1882 | M |

Cheyenne River Census 1913

805	Black Shawl		1845	F
2260	Russell Red Horse		Husb	1882	M
2261	Ellen Bear Growling	White Buffalo	Wife	1869	F

Cheyenne River Census 1914

2248	Russell Red Horse		Husb	1882	M
2249	Ellen Bear Growling (White Buffalo)		Wife	1869	F
119	Black Shawk			1845	F

Cheyenne River Census 1915

2002	Red Horse, Russell		Hus	1882	M
2003	Ellen Bear Growling		Wife	1869	F
	309				
	Black Shawl			71	F

Cheyenne River Census 1916

	843				
	Russell Red Horse			34	M
	Ellen Bear Crawling (White Buffalo)		Wife	47	F
	Tk. 309				
781	Black Shawl			1845	F

Cheyenne River Census 1917

790	Black Shawl		Wid.	1845	F
	Tk. 843				
2219	Russell Red Horse		Husb	1882	M
2220	Ellen Bear Growling (White Buffalo)		Wife	1869	F

Cheyenne River Census 1918

	Tk 309				
693	Black Shawl			1845	F
	tTk 843				
2013	Russell Red Horse			1882	M
2014	Ellen Bear Growling (White Buffalo)		Wife	1869	F

Cheyenne River Census 1919

	309				
699	Black Shawl			1845	F
	843				
1978	Russell Red Horse			1882	M
1979	Ellen Bear Growling		wife	1869	F

Cheyenne River Census 1920

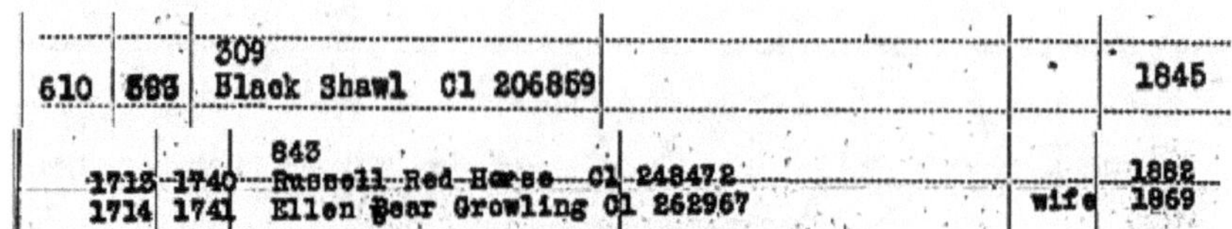

Cheyenne River Census 1924

Cheyenne River Census 1925   (Russell missing)

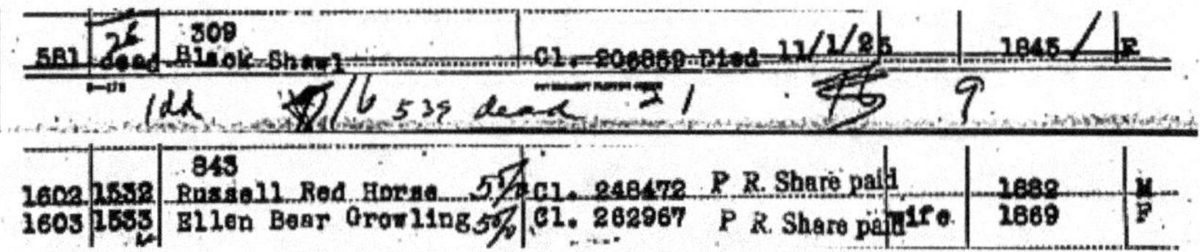

Cheyenne River Census 1926   (Black Shawl is dead, in this record)

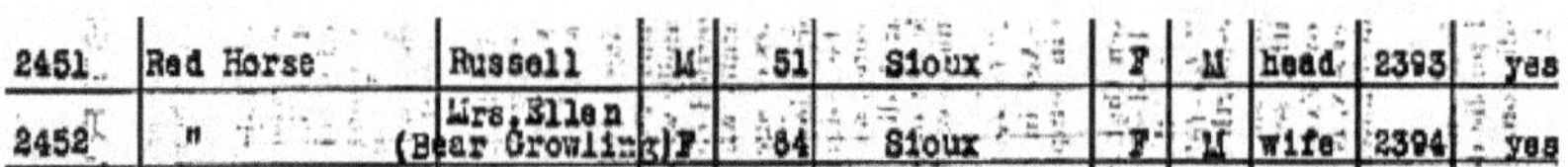

Cheyenne River Census 1930

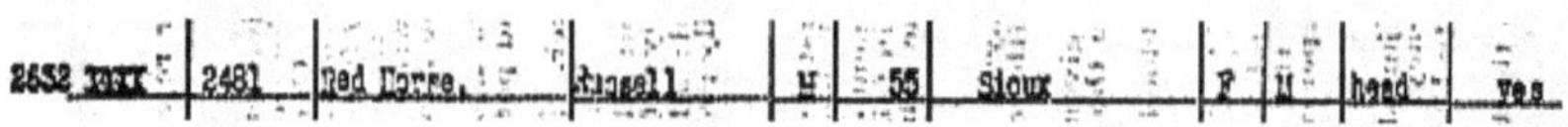

Cheyenne River Census 1933

Cheyenne River Census 1937

State __North Dakota__ Reservation __Cheyenne River__ Agency or Jurisdiction __Cheyenne Agency__

Deaths occurring between the dates of July 1, 1925 and June 30, 1926 of Indians enrolled at Jurisdiction

Fill in dates in blank space provided above. The current year Death Roll must cover same date as Census Roll.

Number on last Census Roll		Name		Date of death			Age at death	Sex	Tribe	Ward	Degree of blood	Cause of death	At jurisdiction where enrolled (yes or no)
Year	Number	Surname	Given	Year	Month	Day							
1925	468	Another Day or Blue Day,	Alice	1926	Jan.	6	83	F	C. R. Sioux		F	Unknown	Yes
1925	801	Arpan,	Ellen	1926	Jan.	14	14	M	C. R. Sioux		½ F.	A'Gratis	Yes
	None	Bald Eagle,	Archie	1926	Mar.	4	7/12	M	C. R. Sioux		F	Pneumonia	Yes
1925	2014	Bears In The Eye,	Robert	1926	Apr.	28	28	M	C. R. Sioux		F	Tuberculosis	Yes
1925	183	Bear Stands Straight,	Abraham	1926	June	1	91	M	C. R. Sioux		F	General Senility	Yes
	None	Black Bull,	Evangeline	1925	Dec.	19	11 days	F	C. R. Sioux		F	Not Stated	Yes
1924	1706	Black Bull,	Peter	1925	Dec.	19	8	M	C. R. Sioux		F	Unknown	Yes
1925	661	Black Shawl		1925	Nov.	3	80	F	C. R. Sioux		F	Unknown	Yes

Record of Black Shawl's death 1925, Cheyenne River Reservation

List of White & other persons registered at Rosebud

Date	Name	Age	(married or single)	Occupation	Birthplace	Residence
1880				Laborer	Missouri	Dakota
June 3	Joseph H. Ladour	36	M	Laborer	Missouri	Dakota
" "	Wm McLune	31	S	Surveyor artist	East Indies	Dakota
	John Marshall	36	M	Surveyor artist	Ireland	do

White and "other persons" in Census rolls

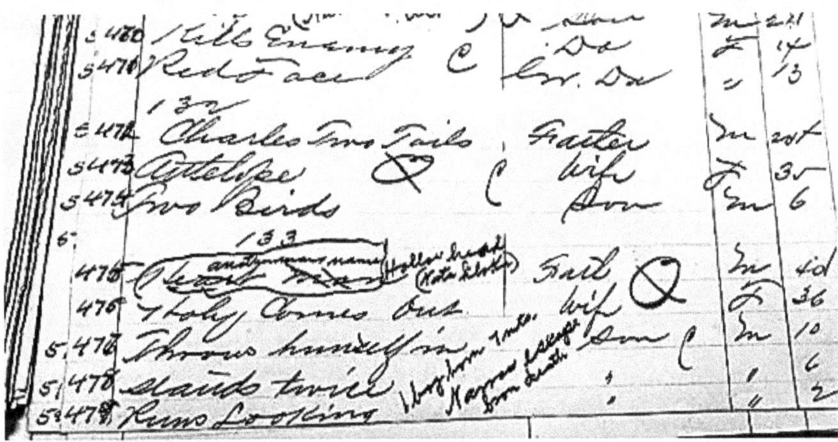

Chatty addendum about a boy who had a "narrow escape from death" in Census Rolls

SELECT BIBLIOGRAPHY

Ambrose, Stephen	*Custer and Crazy Horse*
Blanchard, Julia	*McGillycuddy, Agent*
Blevins, Will	*Stone Song*
Blevins, Will	*Raven Shadow*
Blevins, Will	*The Rock Child*
Blevins, Will	*Rendezvous* Series 1-6
Blevins, Will	*Charbonneau*
Brave Bird, Mary	*Ohitika Woman*
Bray, Kingsley	*Crazy Horse: A Lakota Life*
Brininstool, E. Alonzo	*Red Cloud: The Great Ogllala Sioux War Chief*
Brown, Bruce	*Crazy Horse at War*
Brown, Bruce	*100 Voices from the Little Bighorn*
Brown, Dee	*Bury My Heart at Wounded Knee*
Brown, Dee	*Creek Mary's Blood*
Brown, Dee	*The Fetterman Massacre: Fort Phil Kearny and the Battle of the 100 Slain*
Bunnell, David Hugh	*Good Friday on the Rez*
Catches, Pete	*Sacred Fireplace: Oceti Wakan*
Clark, Robert A.	*The Killing of Chief Crazy Horse*
Clown, Edward	*Crazy Horse: The Lakota Warrior's Life & Legacy*
Cody, William F.	*The Adventures of Buffalo Bill*
Copeland, Martin	*Lame Deer: Memoirs of a Sioux Medicine Man*
Crow Dog, Mary	*Lakota Woman*
Curtis, Edward	*The North American Indian*
Deloria, Vine	*Custer Died for Your Sins*
Eagleman, Ed McGaa	*Black Elk Speaks IV*
Eastman, Charles	*The Soul of the Indian*
Enss, Chris	*Tales behind the Tombstones*
Geronimo	*Geronimo's Story of His Life*
Grouard, Frank	*Legend: Life and Adventures of Frank Grouard*

Gwynne, S. C.   *Empire of the Summer Moon*

Hamalainent, Pekka   *The Comanche Empire*

Hardorff, Richard G.   *The Death of Crazy Horse*

Hicks, Brian   *Toward the Setting Sun: John Ross, The Cherokees and the Trail of Tears*

Hill, Ruth Beebe   *Hanta Yo*

Johnston, Charles H.   *Sitting Bull and Crazy Horse*

King, Thomas   *The Inconvenient Indian*

LaPointe, Ernie   *Sitting Bull: His Life & Legacy*

Least Heat-Moon, W.   *Blue Highways*

Lehmann, Herman   *Nine Years among the Indians*

Marshall III, Joseph M. *The Journey of Crazy Horse: A Lakota History*

Matthiessen, Peter   *In the Spirit of Crazy Horse*

McMurtry, Larry   *Crazy Horse*

Michno, Gregory F.   *Lakota Noon*

Moulton, Candy   *Valentine T. McGillycuddy*

Niehardt, John G.   *Black Elk Speaks*

Orange, Tommy   *There There*

Pember, Mary   *Intergenerational Trauma: Understanding Natives' Inherited Pain*

Philbrick, Nathaniel   *The Last Stand*

Sandoz, Marie   *Crazy Horse, the Strange Man of the Oglalas*

Sargent, Pamela   *Climb the Wind: A Journey into Another Past*

Schilling, Vincent   *Fight the Power: Heroes of Native Resistance*

St. Pierre, Mark   *Walking in the Sacred Manner*

St. Pierre, Mark   *Madonna Swan: A Lakota Woman's Story*

Standing Bear, Luther   *My People, the Sioux*

Steinbeck, John   *Travels with Charlie in Search of America*

Treuer, David   *The Heartbeat of Wounded Knee*

Tyon, Leroy   *The Unrelented: The Untold Story*

Weatherford, Jack   *Native Roots: How the Indians Enriched America*

Wilson, James   *The Earth Shall Weep: A History of Native America*

SOME LAKOTA WORDS

Ahte:	father
Akicita:	traditional Lakota tribal police
Blotahunka:	advisors to a large war party
Bo-ton-ton:	confusion
Canku Luta:	Red Road
Canpahmiyan:	rolling wood (for covered wagon)
Cante wasta upo:	welcome with an open heart
Cannupa Wakan:	sacred pipe
Catkuta:	seat of honor
Cinye:	older brother
Cuwe:	older sister
Dakota:	actual name of the Sioux
Hunkayapi:	making a non-relative a relative; deliberately taking responsibility for another person, mutually
Hanble-ceya:	crying for a vision
Hanta yo:	clear the way
Hau:	I am listening
Heeyay pila maya:	ceremonial thanks
Heyoka:	holy clowns, inspired by the thunder beings
Ho yay:	agreement
Huhukahnigapi:	voting stick
Hunka:	relative/brother by choice
Ihambleiciyapi:	vision quest
Iktomi:	spider, trickster
Ina:	mother
Inipi:	sweat lodge
Inyan:	stone
Itancan:	leader of any group
Iyotanyapi:	honorable
Kiwani owapi:	winter count, Dakota historical calendar
Kola:	brother

Mahapiya Luta:	Red Cloud
Maka:	earth
Maka unchi:	Grandmother Earth
Mato Paha:	Bear Butte
Misun:	younger brother
Mitakuye oyasin:	we are all one
Mitaoyate:	all my relatives
O:	prefix indicates chief or original
Paha Sapa:	Black Hills
Pezuta/pezuta-wicasa:	healer
Pi:	suffix makes word/phrase plural
Pila maya:	thank you
Pta/pte:	male/female buffalo/bison
Ptasapa:	black male buffalo/bison
Ptesanwin:	white buffalo woman (brought the Dakota their moral code)
Saiela:	Cheyenne language (literally, they-talk-red)
Skan:	choice
Tacante canku:	spiritual hoop encircling the Black Hills
Tagoza:	grandchild
Tanka:	younger sister
Tanke:	older sister
Tasunko	Witko: Crazy Horse
Tatanka:	buffalo/bison
Tatanka	Yotake: Sitting Bull
Tecihila:	I love you
Thievo:	white man (in Comanche)
Titonwan:	they-roam-the-plains
Tiyospaye:	family or affinal relatives
Toksha akhay:	farewell till we meet again
Tunkasila:	grandfather
Unci:	grandmother
Waglula:	worm
Wahpani iciya wo:	give away everything

Wakan:	mystery, unknown
Wakan Tanka:	Great Spirit/Great Mystery/ Unknowable
Wakantica/wapiya:	seer
Wakan witkotkoka:	crazy in a sacred way
Wakicun:	decider
Wakinyan:	Wakinyan: thunder beings, lightning
Wakinyan hoton:	thunder
Wambli:	eagle
Wambli Gleska:	spotted eagle, immature eagle
Wambli Tokahe:	Leading Eagle
Wanagi yuha:	spirit owner
Wasicu:	white man (literally, the greedy one)
Wasicu Wakan:	holy white man
Waste/wasteste:	good/very good
Wicasa:	man
Wicasa iyotanyapi:	man of honor
Wicasa Wakan:	holy man/medicine man
Wicasa Itancan:	chief
Win:	woman/girl (makes word or phrase feminine)
Winkte:	hermaphrodite
Witko:	crazy
Wiwanyag wacipi:	Sundance ceremony
Woksapa:	wisdom

SOME OF THE 500 NATIONS

Absaroka/Psa:	Crow
Arapaho:	Blue Clouds/Kiowa/Mahpiyato
Hahatonwan:	Ojibwa/Chippewa
Ihanktonwan:	Yankton Dakotas
Itazipicola:	Sans Arc Dakotas
Kangi:	Dakota name for Crows
Kuya Wicasa:	Lower Brule Sicangu
Minikayawozupi:	Minniconjou Dakotas
Oyateyamni:	Ponca
Padani/Palani:	Dakota name for Arikara/Ree
Pani:	Dakota name for Pawnee
Sahiela:	Cheyenne
Shoshoni:	Snakes
Sicangu:	Burnt Thighs
Sinagleglega:	Navajo
Sintehla Wicasa:	Comanche/rattlesnake man
Sioux:	French contraction of Ojibwe "naduesiu," for snake or enemy (used for the Dakotas)
Titunwan:	Tetons
Tiyataonwan:	original name of Oglalas (they-stay-in-their-camp)
Wazaza:	Osage Dakotas
Witankautahipi:	Santee name for Tetons
Witapaha:	Kiowa

SOME PLACE AND RIVER NAMES

Bad River:	Tricky River/Titon River/Shicha Wakpa
Bear Butte:	Big Butte/Grizzly Butte/Teaching Hill
Big Horn Mountains:	Snowy Hills/White Hills/Shining Mountains
Cannonball River, ND:	River of water-worn stones
Cedar Creek:	Big Stones River - south fork of Cannonball River
Cheyenne River:	Good River
Devil's Tower:	Gray Horn Butte
Grand River:	Palani River/Bigger-than-you-see River
James River:	Dakota River/Yellowish Whitewood River
Lame Deer River, MT:	Muddy Creek
Laramie River:	Swimming-bird River
Little Bighorn River:	Greasy Grass River/Fat Grass River
Little Missouri River, ND:	River of Pronghorn Pits
Mississippi River:	River of Canoes
Missouri River:	Big River/Muddy River/Mud Water
Moreau River:	Owl River
Niobara River:	Running Water
North Platte River:	Flat-water River/Shell River/Shell-on the-neck (= clams) River
Powder River:	Shifting Sands River/Dust River
Reno Creek:	Buffalo Creek/Ash Creek
Rosebud Valley:	Red Flower Creek
Sand Creek, Colorado:	Black Lake/Briny Lake
South Platte River:	Fat-meat River
Thunder Butte:	Flying-mystery Butte
Tongue River:	Pte-tongue River/Beaver Tail River
Turtle Butte:	Keya Paha River/Hanging Woman Creek
Whetstone Creek:	Izuza Wakhpala
White River:	Earth-smoke River/Maka Izita Wakpa
Yellowstone River:	Branched-horn River/Elk River